As the nation slowly turns its eyes t
on families all too often gets lost in
us that mental illness affects everyone, but no more so than family members and loved ones.

Ms. Malone both thoughtfully and beautifully tells her family's tragic story of loss and redemption as she grieves the untimely loss of her husband at the hands of her son's own mental illness. *Psychotic Rage!* provides the reader with invaluable information pertaining to mental health and wellness that is easy to read and understand. And Ms. Malone puts the issue of mental illness in a much broader context as she explores in great detail the shortcomings of the criminal justice and mental health care delivery systems.

Psychotic Rage! is a must-read for anyone touched by severe and persistent mental illness. As a longtime mental health professional, I offer my compliments to Ms. Malone for writing such a needed and timely book.

Glenn D. Urbach, LMSW
Executive Director
National Alliance on Mental Illness
Houston, Texas

This book is so relevant to the many families with loved ones struggling with mental illness. Benny bravely shares her story of hope and despair in a loving and compassionate voice. *Psychotic Rage!* is a must-read for families, therapists, school counselors, teachers, and clergy.

Robbie Burnett, Ph.D.
Licensed Professional Counselor

It is rare that one book could have such broad appeal to multiple populations. *Psychotic Rage!* speaks to families who are experiencing the multitude of stressors related to chronic mental illness. It is an excellent resource for mental health professionals and students who are in mental health training programs. It also provides insight into the need for reframing the lens through which we view mental illness and the need for advocacy efforts to restructure the current public and private systems related to mental illness.

Malone tells her personal story from the positions of a loving mother, a counseling professional, and an advocate. The book gripped me from the first chapter. Her descriptions of the signs and symptoms of her son's illness and the impact it had on his functioning provides invaluable insight into the daily life of a patient and a family. Malone's description of psychosis is one of the best explanations I have ever read. The inclusion of Chris's journal entries also provides an intimate look at the psychotic perspective.

As a Counselor Educator, this will be assigned reading for my students. Thank you, Benny, for sharing your personal turmoil and trauma for the benefit of others.

Le'Ann L. Solmonson, Ph.D., LPC-S, CSC
Director of Counselor Education Programs
Associate Professor
Stephen F. Austin State University
President, Texas Counseling Association, 2014-15

Benny Malone's story shines a beacon of hope into the dark world of mental illness. Through her story, she has opened a door into a heart-wrenching reality, and has done so with compassion, respect, and gentleness. Reading this book will open your heart, enlighten your understanding, and equip you with tools and resources you need to move forward.

Casandra Martin
Author of the Women Opening the World Bible Study Series

Ms. Malone has written a gut-wrenching account of living with a mentally ill family member and what it is like to navigate mental health services and the legal system in our country. From the first indication of her son's mental illness in his early teens to the murder of his own father in his mid-twenties, we are struck by the day-to-day hope, fears, and sheer exhaustion that mental illness can bring to the entire family system. This family's ordeal most likely plays out in other homes in our nation, and, for this reason, we can be grateful for this book which advocates for a more compassionate and efficient way of assisting families who are struggling with mental illness. This is a "must read" for everyone because all of us must be invested in revamping social services and the judicial system to treat the mentally ill with the dignity and compassion that we would want for our own son or daughter.

Judith A. Nelson, Ph.D., LPC-S, LMFT

And the Best Endorsement of All to Me:

Mom, your book is well written. It is pretty much on target if someone wants to know what it is like to be me, a person with a severe mental illness.

Chris Malone

One foot in front of the other... Always! Benny Malone

Psychotic Rage!

A True Story of Mental Illness, Murder, and Reconciliation

Benny Malone

Foreword by Dr. Scott Poland

Bedford, Texas

Psychotic Rage!

Published in association with Creative Enterprises Studio, A Premier Publishing Services Group, PO Box 224, Bedford, TX 76095. CreativeEnterprisesStudio.com.

Please note that while this is a true story, some names have been changed to protect the privacy of the individuals.

Library of Congress Control Number: 2014941796

ISBN: 978-0-9911889-2-5

Cover Design: Anneli Anderson, AnneliStudio.com
Interior Design: Inside-Out Design & Typesetting

Printed in the United States of America
14 15 16 17 18 19 MG 6 5 4 3 2 1

This book is dedicated to my sons, Will and Chris. We are a much smaller family now than we were when Chris began experiencing symptoms of mental illness almost twenty years ago. I pray the loving bond that still exists among the three of us continues in accord with God's Word in 1 Corinthians 13:7.

Love never gives up, never loses faith, is always hopeful,
and endures through every circumstance.

Contents

Contents

Part Three
Passage to Young Adulthood

Part Four
My Next Journey

Part Five
What I Learned That Might Help You

Contents

Foreword

June 29, 2005: I had recently retired as the Director of Psychological Services for Cypress-Fairbanks Independent School District in Texas and had just moved to Florida for my new faculty position at a university. I remember thinking how shocked I was to hear that Chris Malone, the twenty-four-year-old son of Rob and Benny Malone, had attacked them and had killed his father.

My specialty is crisis intervention. I had led most of the crisis interventions in the school district for twenty-four years and had even led national teams in the aftermath of tragedies, such as Columbine. I immediately felt saddened by the tragic news and wished I could have been there to offer support to Benny. Not only had she lost her husband and best friend, Rob, she knew her son Chris would certainly be incarcerated.

Benny was someone I personally worked with when she first became a teacher, then a counselor, and later an administrator in the district. Benny is a special person and the teacher and counselor that everyone wishes their child could have! Benny was also the primary organizer and a trainer for all the parenting classes in the district. She had talked with me many times about all the difficulties Chris was experiencing and the roller coaster ride from the age of fourteen into adulthood.

As a psychologist in Texas, I was well aware of the shortcomings of the mental health services that were available and the challenges parents faced when they had a mentally ill child. I knew Benny and Rob were well suited to be advocates for Chris and they would make extraordinary efforts to get Chris the help that he needed.

Foreword

I am honored to write the Foreword to this exceptional book and freely admit I cried when I read the details of the tragedy, but I also marveled at the strength Benny found in her faith and her ability to forgive her son. Benny knows her husband would want her to forgive Chris. I am reminded of the Ernest Hemingway quote, "The world breaks everyone, but afterward many are stronger at the broken places." Benny Malone is a stronger person and has shared her story so that others who have family members struggling with mental illness can learn from what her family has been through.

An excellent writer and with a great memory for details, Benny describes the progression of her son's mental illness and his battles with substance abuse. Chris was hospitalized ten times in a nine-year period and diagnosed with schizoaffective disorder in which his core belief system was bounded by paranoia and mistrust. She describes the treatment he received and also the time he spent in the Harris County jail. Chris was finally found not guilty by reason of insanity for the murder of his father in 2011.

Mental illness is a disease that is not well understood, and there needs to be more resources devoted to improving treatment for the mentally ill. Benny's book provides many important tips and resources for those who have family members struggling with mental illness. She is hopeful for future treatments that will improve the quality of life for everyone suffering from mental illness.

Scott Poland, PhD
Faculty and Co-Director, Suicide and Violence Prevention Office
Nova Southeastern University, Fort Lauderdale, Florida

Dr. Scott Poland is a licensed psychologist and the author of numerous books and articles about school crisis and youth violence. He previously was selected as the Most Outstanding Psychologist in Texas and also served as the President of the National Association of School Psychologists.

Acknowledgments

Two very special groups traveled with me on this long journey of my younger son's mental illness, and I want to acknowledge their love, support, special knowledge, talents, and skills.

All the professional counselors who have encouraged me and enlightened my life and the lives of many others like me who strive to help those we love as they struggle daily with mental illness.

My inner circle
—you know who you are—
you have been on this journey with me for many years and still never resist a call for help. God is adding stars to your crown!

Introduction

It has been nine years since my husband's death at the hands of our mentally ill son. Only recently have I decided to publicly tell the story of our difficult journey with his mental illness in the hope that others may benefit from this frontline description of our experience. My husband, Rob, and I were well-educated, healthy, loving partners rearing two smart, handsome young sons in a suburban neighborhood of Houston, Texas. You might think all would have been well with the Malone family, but it wasn't.

The eleven years of our lives prior to Rob's death in 2005 were spent riding a terrifying roller coaster of mental illness. We endured many up-and-down periods of diagnosis, treatment, hope, despair, crisis, hospitalization, stabilization, suicide attempts, fear, and, finally, our younger son's unexpected and unbelievable moment of psychotic rage that ended Rob's life. What happened during a few minutes on a summer afternoon at home still impacts my family in an immense way.

Some of the issues surrounding our son Chris's diagnosed illness—schizoaffective disorder, bipolar type—and the years of treatment prior to this horrific event continue to distress me, but I still take one day at a time and am at peace, knowing I am not now and never was in control of Chris's illness. My hope is that those who read our story will gain a better understanding of mental illness and the vast impact it has on so many lives, both those who are ill as well as those who are not. If you are one of the many family members who have a loved one who is mentally ill, I hope you find support and comfort and are enriched by learning about resources that are available to you. If you are a mental health professional or are training in this field, I hope you will gain insight into the repetitive but unpredictable challenges faced by your clients and the families that love them. If you are a community member, policy maker, or local, state, or national leader, I hope you will grasp the enormous social cost in pain and suffering and in financial inefficiencies inherent in our system of inadequate services for persons who are mentally ill. If you are poor in spirit or one who mourns, I hope you will gain encouragement as you make your own journey toward healing. You are not alone.

Part One

PAIN, SHOCK, THEN NUMBNESS

1

Psychosis on a Summer Afternoon

On Wednesday, June 29, 2005, shortly after 1:00 p.m., my son Chris Malone assaulted me and stabbed his father to death in a moment of psychotic rage. He was twenty-four years old, and his dad and I were both fifty-nine years old. The charge of *instant event,* the legal term used to describe Chris's act of murder, was filed against him by the Harris County District Attorney on the following day, June 30, 2005.

On that summer afternoon of the "instant event," I was on day three of my summer vacation, my between-the-school-years two-week break from my job as a central office guidance and counseling administrator in a large suburban school district. It was shortly after noon, and I was in the kitchen putting dishes in the dishwasher when my husband, Rob, arrived home from his morning of teaching summer school at a local college. He poured himself a cup of coffee and sat down at the dining table to visit with me. We were sharing about our mornings, laughing and feeling at ease. I told Rob that the college president's secretary had called earlier and left a message for him to call back for an appointment with the president regarding a new position in the economics department for which Rob had applied. He had already completed the rounds of department interviews, and this one would be the last and, he hoped, the one with the new job offer. He returned the secretary's call and was excited when he got off the phone. The call left him feeling encouraged and hopeful. Good news was sometimes a hard thing to come by in our household, and we were probably acting a little silly. We just felt happy and blessed.

Rob returned to his chair and cup of coffee in the dining room and began to tell me everything the secretary had said on the phone. I went back to loading dishes into the dishwasher. As Rob was telling me about his upcoming appointment, Chris quietly walked around the corner from our living room into the kitchen. He stood there, and as our dog, Pepper, walked over to greet him, he kicked at her. Seeing this unexpected move by Chris, I said, "Did you kick the dog?" Without uttering a word and in a move I did not see but will never forget, Chris slugged me in the face, his fist breaking four facial bones and knocking me unconscious to the floor in front of the refrigerator.

Rob rushed to my defense as I was lying unconscious on the kitchen floor. Within moments I became aware that they were straddling me and fighting. All this was surreal. I could not see because blood was streaming into my eyes from a gash on my forehead. My glasses had smashed into my face when I hit the floor. I could not find them anywhere on the floor around me. I was totally in survival and flight mode. I felt an intense urgency to crawl out from under these two men standing and fighting above me. I was scared and in pain, but even so part of my brain was worrying that they would stumble, fall, and get hurt.

Rob managed to wrestle Chris across the kitchen and pinned him against the kitchen cabinet as I scooted out from under them. I was struggling to stand and regain my wits. I felt totally blinded by the blood streaming into my eyes and was grasping for something to wipe my face. I was also still trying to find my glasses, which were absolutely essential to me. Then I heard Rob yell, "He's got a knife. He's got a knife!" I never saw what happened next.

Chris apparently had grabbed a small knife that must have been on the countertop. He reached over Rob's shoulder and plunged it into his back. It was just a little knife, but it punctured a lung. When I was able to focus, I saw Rob leaning forward over the kitchen sink. Chris was no longer in the kitchen. I didn't know where he was. I did not see blood on Rob's back, nor did I see a tear or cut in his blue dress shirt. I did not see a bloody knife or blood on the floor or cabinet. I went over to him. He said, "It's bad; it's bad."

I had a kitchen towel in my hand and started to press it against his back, still not seeing any injury. Intuitively, I must have realized that Rob had been stabbed, but he did not tell me that, and I couldn't see well enough to know what had actually happened.

As I was struggling to help my husband, I was also madly attempting to dial 911 on our cordless phone. Again, my poor vision, no glasses, and blood in my eyes along with the trauma of what had just happened tangled my fingers, and I could not make that simple little call. I ran outside into the front yard hoping to see a neighbor, yardman, anyone who could help me dial 911. The street was eerily quiet, calm, and peaceful, with no one out and about. It was a pretty, breezy summer afternoon, a world away from mine at that moment. I ran back inside the house and found Rob struggling to breathe and still standing at the sink, leaning heavily into it. I rushed to support and hold him, forgetting the phone. I felt so desperate. With my foot I managed to pull a kitchen chair close to Rob and helped him sit down. When I tried the 911 call again, those three little numbers mercifully connected for me.

It is so frustrating to try to explain a true emergency to someone on the telephone that cannot see what is going on. The operator wanted me to speak calmly and asked me to repeat what was happening. She did speak calmly to me, and that eventually helped me calm down. She told me to help Rob lie down on the floor on his side. After I helped him to the floor as the operator told me, his breathing became more labored. He said, "That's worse. I can't breathe." I lifted him back into the chair. She told me that help was on the way and began to ask me how the stabbing had occurred. She wanted to know where Chris was and if he was still armed. I told her I didn't know. I had not seen him armed and could not see Rob's injury. I did not know that my sweet, smart, clever husband's last words to me would be, "I can't breathe."

Help Arrives

As I stood beside Rob, holding on to the phone like a lifeline, I began to hear a siren. The next thing I heard was a loud, gruff male voice shouting at the front of the house. A police officer with his gun extended came cautiously into the kitchen where Rob and I were. I was still holding the phone and dripping blood from my forehead. Rob was panting and gasping for breath. The officer put his gun away and called for the paramedics to come in. They apparently were not allowed to enter before he checked the safety of the residence.

The paramedics quickly began to assess Rob. Someone was moving furniture in the living room, and a stretcher was rolled in. Another paramedic took me by the arm and led me to a corner of the living room. He spoke softly to me and wrapped my head with a large bandage. Thankfully the bleeding into my eyes finally stopped. He left me huddled down in the corner, shaking and shivering. Without my glasses, I still could not see well. I knew there was a group of blue-uniformed people bending over what I thought was a stretcher with Rob on it. I overheard someone quietly comment, "I can't get a pulse." I was so scared. I became aware of my face and head throbbing and my body trembling and feeling totally weak. There was a rush past me. The paramedics were rolling Rob out to an ambulance. No one spoke to me about his condition or told me where they were

There was a rush past me. The paramedics were rolling Rob out to an ambulance. No one spoke to me about his condition or told me where they were taking him. They were all business. Rob was their total concern. I have never felt so alone.

taking him. They were all business. Rob was their total concern. I have never felt so alone.

After a few minutes a paramedic helped me stand up and walked me out to another waiting ambulance. The sun was so bright! I saw many police cars and two ambulances parked in front of my house. There were people standing in the yards around my house. I could not see them clearly and have no idea who they were. One police car seemed to be blocking my street. Just moments after I entered an ambulance, I heard the other one leave with its siren at full blast. I lay down on the stretcher and asked where they were taking Rob. The paramedic told me the name of the nearby hospital. The paramedic then left, and I waited alone in the ambulance for what felt like a very long time. Perhaps it was only five or ten minutes. I don't know. While alone and waiting in the ambulance, I kept thinking about the "can't get a pulse" comment by the paramedic attending to Rob and began to feel panicky.

When an attendant finally came back to the ambulance, I asked for an ice pack for my face. I also asked the attendant to bring me my purse and my cell phone. They were still in the house. I was desperate to call my older son, Will, my brother, Steve, a friend, and a coworker—anyone who could help me. I'm sure I was in shock, but my brain was racing, and I felt so helpless, so out of communication, so unaware of what was happening to all three of us. I also had the sense that I was an aside to this event. The attendant had seemed surprised when I had asked for an ice pack. Briefly I thought about me and wondered how badly I was hurt. I could tell my face was swelling a lot, and my head was aching and throbbing as if it were being jackhammered. I realized that no one had even checked my blood pressure, and they had just left me alone in the ambulance for that period of time. Much later I figured out that Chris had become everyone's focus as Rob's ambulance sped away.

Eventually someone brought my purse and cell phone to me. I called a very close friend first. My son was working out of town on a commercial construction site in Victoria, and I did not know how to get in touch with him. I briefly told my friend what had taken place and asked her to call Will but to hold back on telling him over the phone the details of what had actually happened. I wanted her to tell him that his dad was in the hospital and that I needed him to come and be with me. I was worried about Will's reaction and his driving like a wild man the two hundred miles back home to Houston. I also asked my friend to call my brother, Steve, for me. I did not have many phone numbers in my cell phone contacts list in 2005. I knew she could find his phone number and make the call. Until that sunny summer afternoon, I had primarily used my cell phone to call my family and say, "I'm on my way home! See you soon."

2

The Hospital

Just as paramedics entered my ambulance to take me to the hospital, a third ambulance pulled up in front of my house. They told me I needed to move to the new ambulance because Chris was also being transported. I didn't understand why but was told that he was going to a different hospital than the one where Rob and I were going. I was moved by stretcher, for which I was very thankful. The attack had been about thirty minutes earlier, so shock was setting in, and I was now feeling very weak. During the transfer from one ambulance to the other, a television news crew rushed up to videotape me. The wonderfully kind paramedic pushing my gurney shielded my face with his notepad. It made me angry that the media was invading my family's privacy.

The trip to the hospital took about fifteen minutes. It wasn't far from our house. The ambulance pulled up to a temporary entrance to the emergency room. Apparently construction was under way in that part of the hospital. I remember that it was very dusty, and the wind was blowing.

After I was rolled into the ER, my stretcher was parked in the hallway. The paramedic left me alone to complete the admission. It was quiet, and I tried to look around the area for some view of Rob on his stretcher. I didn't see anyone except my paramedic and a nurse talking at the nurses' station. Then a doctor came over to me and leaned on the rails of the gurney. I felt relieved to see him and asked, "How's my husband?" He answered with no prelude, "He died." That's it. That is all he said. "He died."

I began to scream, "No, no, no!" Probably twenty-five times I screamed that word as I kicked my legs and shook my head in a fury. I don't know what happened to the doctor after he said those two words. I never saw him again. A woman, who turned out to be an employee of the hospital admissions and insurance department, pulled my stretcher over to a corner in a more secluded area of the hallway. She stayed with me and spoke softly as she patted me on my arm. I eventually exhausted myself and just cried.

I gave all my chaos to her, and she took charge. It was exactly what I wanted and needed as my world spun totally out of control.

The next few minutes are not part of my memory bank. After a while I realized I had been moved to an ER room and was in a bed instead of on a stretcher. A nurse had put a blood pressure cuff on my arm and was hooking up an IV. Then a wonderful thing happened. One of my best friends walked in the door. She and I are not only very close, longtime friends, but we also worked together in my school district, where she was a top administrator. She was the first angel God sent to me. I gave all my chaos to her, and she took charge. It was exactly what I wanted and needed as my world spun totally out of control.

"You Need to Come"

Shortly, two more of my best friends arrived. Now there were three of them and one of me. What a comfort! The message that my friends Betty, Sharon, and Sadie had received was, "Benny is at the hospital. You need to come." I do not know how the story spread so quickly, but it did. A neighbor a couple of streets over from my house was friends with Sharon's daughter and had called her to ask if she knew anything about the police cars and ambulances at the

Malones' house. Sharon's daughter called her mother. Sharon quickly called Betty, who told her to come to the hospital. Sadie was the friend I had first called and asked to notify Will and my brother when I was waiting in the ambulance. Before searching for their phone numbers, she quickly called Betty at her office because Betty worked just across the street from the hospital.

My brother's wife, Patty, had stopped at the grocery store on the way home from work and received a cell phone call from a mutual friend of ours. Apparently the television news station that had been at the house had already released some information. The mutual friend told Patty what she had seen and heard on TV—that a stabbing had occurred at a Malone residence in northwest Houston. Patty and Steve knew something bad had happened before they received the call from Sadie. Sadie told them where to go, and they quickly left home for the one-hour drive across town.

My friends and family thought something very bad had happened to Chris. Seeing me with my head bandaged in the ER did not make sense to them. This close circle of friends and family had kept vigil with Rob and me during many close calls with Chris. They were supportive and loving, but, like me, they never anticipated an event like this.

My ER room was quiet. The nurses walked softly and spoke softly. One nurse stitched up the gash on my forehead. A doctor ordered a CT scan of my head. A sheriff's detective came in and took pictures of my face and asked me some questions about what had happened. He, too, was kind and soft-spoken. After he left, I asked to see a mirror so I could look at my face. The entire left side was puffy and swollen from forehead to chin and dark blue-black in color. My left eye was swollen shut. I looked really bad! It was a shock to see myself. Seeing the extent of the injury to my face reinforced the reality of everything that had happened. Those around me in the ER clearly were ahead of me in the reality department. I needed quiet, and that's what they gave me.

Sweet, numb quiet.

Family

After being in the hospital for about three hours, more people began to come by. I received some phone calls, which Betty, Sharon, or Sadie took. They also managed to get in touch with Rob's eighty-three-year-old father, Robert, who lived in a small town about an hour north of Houston. He was told there had been an accident and I wanted him to come to the hospital. After a while I began to worry about him because he had a poor memory, would often get lost, and was not comfortable driving in the big city. He had a cell phone but did not know how to use it well. He did not answer whenever we tried to call and check on him. Finally, about two hours after he had left home, he called to say he was lost. It turned out that he was close to the hospital and was able to follow Betty's directions to finally make it safely to where we were.

Telling my father-in-law what had happened was difficult. He and my husband were very close. They had recently taken a bird-watching trip to Aransas Pass, Texas. Rob had told me it was a special time with his dad. They had shared a room overnight and must have talked all night. Rob said it was as if they were kids having a sleepover, just talking and talking. When I first told Robert that Rob had died, he didn't understand me. He, too, thought something had happened to Chris. I had to repeat myself, and then he just crumpled to the floor. I had lost my spouse. He had lost his child.

The one person I most wanted to see arrived last—my older son, Will. When Will literally burst into the room around 4:00 p.m., he looked huge to me! I jumped out of the bed, and we hugged long and hard. When Will had gotten the phone call to come to the hospital, something in my friend's voice made him think the worst had happened. He knew too much of Chris's history, and he knew that I would have told him if Chris were hurt and that was the reason I was at the hospital. When he saw me in an ER bed without his dad standing beside me, he knew. He knew.

Shades of Gray

After Will got there, the nurse asked me if we would like to see Rob. He was still in a private hospital room near the ER. She explained what we would see when we went in, and then she gave me his watch, wallet, and wedding band. The hospital had to wait for the coroner's office to come. Once a person dies in this kind of situation, the body can't be moved after death until it is released by the coroner. The next step for my good, strong, loving husband would be an autopsy at Harris County morgue.

What did Will and I see? The door to the room was closed. As we walked in, I saw gray. Everything in the room seemed to glow in varying shades of gray. There was no lighting, but it was not dark. Rob lay there just as he must have been when the ER doctor pronounced him dead. He was propped up in a bed. He had a syringe in the center of his chest. A sheet was covering him below the syringe. His eyes were closed. He looked gray too. I sat beside him on one side of the bed. Will stood beside him on the other side. We just looked and were still. I don't remember our saying anything, but perhaps we did. What was there to say?

The nurse had explained that the knife had punctured Rob's lung. All the blood that was returning to his lungs to be reoxygenated in the normal course of life instead pooled in his lungs and consumed the space his heart needed to beat properly. The syringe represented a mighty effort to drain the chest cavity so Rob's heart could beat. Perhaps the effort was too late. I think his heart stopped beating before the ambulance sped away with sirens blaring. How long did it take Rob to die? Not very long. Chris's moment of psychotic rage, from his slugging me to stabbing Rob, lasted no more than ten minutes.

A lot of good things had been happening on my behalf while I was in the ER. Without my knowledge God's angels were busy at work. Al, the husband of my friend Sharon, had been dispatched to my house to survey what was needed. The most obvious need was to do something about the bloody rugs on the floor, blood stains in the kitchen, and general disarray in the living room.

It was clear I could not go home. Al called a local hotel and made reservations for my family and me for the next few nights. He also stayed at the house that evening to keep curiosity seekers away. Crime-scene tape was stretched across the front of my house, and the door had been left unlocked after the police had gone. No one tells you how long crime-scene tape has to stay up. Was there a rule about that? None of us knew.

Al was also there to walk through the house with Will when he came home to see things for himself. A television truck was parked in front and was shining its bright lights on our house as Will walked to the front door. Seeing the media waiting outside and going into our house wrapped with crime tape was tough for Will. He and Al first walked into the kitchen. Will stopped, numb with shock, and softly said, "Wow, this is where it happened." Al stood beside him as they stared at the blood on the floor and cabinets. Al was the perfect man to share those few moments with Will. I am so glad he had Al.

Sadie called my coworkers to get the word out to my fellow counselors and other central office colleagues. She also bought food and snacks to bring to us that night in the hotel.

Sharon went shopping and bought me two dresses, a robe, a nightgown, and underwear. Everything fit!

Another friend went to the one-hour optical shop and ordered me a new pair of glasses. The shop allowed her to use an old prescription that was on file.

After Will and I saw Rob, there was no reason to stay at the hospital. My CT scan did not show a concussion, so I was released by the ER doctor who had examined me. We formed a little caravan of about six cars in the parking lot. I saw many people standing in a semicircle outside near the ER exit. I could not recognize anyone because I did not have on my glasses, and my vision was further impaired by my injury. But I could see them waving, and I knew they were my coworkers and friends. God had sent more angels.

By the time we arrived at the hotel where Al had reserved our rooms, someone had also called my church. The minister and a good friend came to the hotel to visit with me. They prayed with me and comforted me. They did not stay long. The church arranged for a cleaning service to come to the house while we were staying at the hotel, and they paid the cleaning service bill. They also made plans for an after-funeral meal.

My brother called a funeral home to alert them to our need. Because of Steve's call, the funeral director was able to obtain information about the autopsy and how long that would take. The funeral home representative became our link for information from the medical examiner's office and later from the office of the Texas Attorney General Crime Victim's program.

My sister-in-law, Patty, tracked down what had happened with Chris and learned that he would go before a judge the next morning. His ambulance had taken him to a hospital where he received medical and psychiatric evaluations before the police officers transported him to Harris County jail. Why did they do a psychiatric assessment on Chris? Because he had a history of mental health services going years back with Harris County Mental Health and Mental Retardation Authority (MHMRA). Another blessing from God—the police had records, and they checked them. Because of that, Chris was incarcerated in a special area of the jail for inmates with mental illness, the MHMRA forensic unit. His arrest represented the beginning of his longest sustained period of mental health treatment.

Why did they do a psychiatric assessment on Chris? Another blessing from God—the police had records and they checked them. Because of that, Chris was incarcerated in a special area of the jail for inmates with mental illness, the MHMRA forensic unit.

Finally June 29, 2005, came to an end. By then my body, mind, and soul were craving deep, deep rest.

3

The Funeral

I believe funerals are for the living. They fill a human need for communal grieving. My strong faith assured me that Rob was in a good place now. But I was not. *Numb* is the best word to describe me on Thursday, June 30. I just wanted to stay in bed. I don't remember being aware of anything going on around me, but I do know that Steve attended Chris's court arraignment while his wife Patty made phone calls to lawyers and mental health advocates. I still have all their conversation and observation notes from that day. Thus began my learning process about the Texas criminal justice system, specifically in Harris County, that I would soon be immersed in.

I'm glad I was not there with Steve in court that day. Apparently it was a story of some note, because the hearing was filmed, and the *Houston Chronicle* included a big article in the city life section of the newspaper. Pictures of my house and the investigating sheriff's deputies were displayed prominently beside the article.

Interviews with my neighbors and shots of Chris in handcuffs and wearing an orange jail uniform were telecast on TV. Again God showed me mercy when a few days later, on July 7, the London subway bombings pushed the Malone patricide story to the side.

By Friday I was able to leave the hotel room. Steve and Will had already met with the funeral home to make the arrangements, though we still did not know when the autopsy would be completed and Rob's body would be released to the funeral home. The decisions were all made. I just had to give my approval. The only contribution I made was clarifying some historical dates and names for the obituary.

> There is no subtlety in death. It is blunt and in your face.

While the funeral plans were being discussed, I heard or remembered all the words used to describe a dead person—*body, remains, deceased, expired, victim, the lost one, the loved one.* None of those words made sense to me, then or now. It was Rob who was coming back one last time, at least on this earth. Yes, I knew it was only his body. After seeing him one more time, I knew my Rob was no longer present. There is no comparison between how a person looks in life and how he looks in death. There is no subtlety in death. It is blunt and in your face. In contrast, some of the words the world uses regarding a person's death seem silly to me. "You lost your loved one? I'm so sorry. How did you lose him?"—knowing full well that he is lying in a casket you recently picked out for him. "Remains" sounds like something that is left over, not the person you most certainly still love. "Expired" is what I call an out-of-date coupon. As hard as it was to hear, what the doctor first said to me in the ER hallway is the truth: "He died." I've told Will that when I die, he must say, "She died."

Late Friday afternoon we were informed that Rob's body would be released to the funeral home that night. Since the following day was Saturday, we decided to have the visitation and the funeral the next morning. Afternoon would have been better, but the funeral home was already booked. Planning funerals is not like planning a wedding reception or party for which you have time to search out special locations. Some decisions were easy. No one wanted to prolong our coming together to mourn.

I wanted to see Chris before the funeral. I didn't know what he knew. None of the family had been in contact with him or anyone else in the legal system. Steve took me to visit Chris at the jail. What an overwhelming experience that was! It was dirty, smelly, crowded, and loud, and we had to wait a long time. No one informed us of what to expect, and others clearly knew the routine. We did not, but I would learn, and I did, very well.

When Chris appeared, he was escorted into a small, glass-enclosed, concrete-walled room—very thick glass and very thick concrete. His hands were cuffed behind him even though he was in a small section by himself. Behind me was a much larger room into which several prisoners were admitted at one time, all uncuffed and freely moving about. That meant something, but I did not know what at the time. Cut into the thick glass was a small metal-framed hole through which Chris and I attempted to speak to each other. The surrounding noise was almost deafening.

Chris smiled slightly when he saw us. He looked at my bruised, swollen face and asked how I was feeling. He appeared meek and calm and spoke softly. I think he was in shock too. He had learned from news reports and deputies that his dad had died. I told him about the funeral and that it would be the next morning. I asked if he had anything he wanted to tell me. He said, "I loved him. He was my best friend." Then Steve and I left. With deep sighs and our private thoughts, we drove back to the hotel.

Patty, who is an excellent photographer, had an idea for a DVD of music and pictures for the funeral the next day. Not having much time to complete her project, she and a close friend went back to my house while Steve and I were visiting Chris at the jail. Patty wanted to look for Rob's Bible and family pictures. They went into Rob's office to search. As a former corporate economist, college teacher, and extremely avid reader, he had shelves and shelves of books in his small home office. After his wife and children, Rob probably loved books most in this world. Books were stacked on his desk, on the floor, and in a closet. He had a metal storage cabinet squeezed behind the office door that had even more books in it. Pictures were fairly easy for them to find, but they could not locate Rob's Bible. While they were just standing there in his office and looking around, the Bible fell off a shelf behind them. Both Patty and my friend had been looking in another direction, and when it fell, they turned around to see it in plain sight where it had landed on the desk below a shelf. Each asked the other if she had moved the Bible. Neither had seen the book fall. They heard it hit the desk and turned to look. Was the shelf where Rob had placed his Bible wobbly because it was overstacked with books? Did walking up the stairs, moving around the room, or opening the closet door wiggle the book just enough to topple it from its place? I think one of God's unseen angels nudged that Bible so His earthly angels could get on about their business.

Split Loyalties

Everyone got dressed early Saturday morning. By then more family members had come in from out of town. Some were staying at the same hotel with us. I wore one of the dresses that Sharon had bought for me. It felt good to wear something new. It always does. My friend had picked up the new eyeglasses for me, and now I could really see what I looked like. It was not pretty. And my face still hurt. I decided to wear an old pair of prescription sunglasses to the funeral. I felt hidden and that was good.

A lot of people came to Rob's funeral. The chapel was full. It was July 2 and a beautiful, sunny Saturday. Patty's funeral DVD had required many late hours from her the night before, and it was incredible! It was not long, but the pictures, music, and scriptures she incorporated will be with me forever. I saw it play for the first time when I arrived for the visitation at 10:00 a.m. The depiction of our family in the DVD came alive to me. The love we had shared together in our family was vibrantly depicted in the images.

Joel Williams, the minister who preached Rob's funeral service, understood my split loyalties to Rob and Chris. He grasped the confusing challenge before me. I could not get past knowing that I loved both Rob and Chris. Joel beautifully worded the feelings I had expressed to him when he told everyone present that the family "solicits your understanding and even your activism regarding the pervasive, horrific condition that afflicts Chris and others, in hopes of finding relief and healing for others suffering as he suffers . . . Benny is convinced in her heart that if Rob could speak out today he would say, 'Forgive Chris because I love him so much. And please pray that God will cover Chris with His healing and comforting hand in the days to come.' "

I realized that we had been a loving family with strong bonds all around and that it was a terrible, deadly illness named psychosis that left me shattered and grieving today.

Patty's DVD and Joel's words were two more blessings from God. Not only was I lifted up in the moment, but I realized that we had been a loving family with strong bonds all around and that it was a terrible, deadly illness named psychosis that left me shattered and grieving today.

The Death Certificate: "Son's Mental Illness"

About a week later, when I received my ten copies of Rob's death certificate, which the funeral home had ordered for me, I carefully read every word. The cause of death was listed as "Stab wound of back with penetration of lung." One box was checked "Homicide." Another box asked for a description of how the injury occurred. "Stabbed by other person(s)" was the answer.

One box was left blank, but I think a statement should have been included for complete accuracy. That box asked for a listing of other significant conditions contributing to the person's death. I wanted to type, "Son's mental illness."

Part Two

TICKETS FOR THE RIDE

4

Beginning the Ride: Middle School

Rob's death represents the middle of my roller-coaster-ride metaphor, but there is a beginning to my story. At the time we started our ride, I was an elementary school counselor, Rob was a corporate economist, and Chris was a thirteen-year-old in the seventh grade. Our older son, Will, had just begun his freshman year at the University of Texas in Austin. Without a doubt there was stress in our lives. Everyone we knew had stress of one kind or another. But we had joy too, enough to keep our heads up and our hearts smiling.

Sixth Grade: A Great Start

During sixth grade Chris had done well academically. He was in advanced classes for every subject. He also excelled in sports as a star lineman in Little League football. His team, the Klein Jets, had won the division championship in the Little League Super Bowl. Chris was then selected to play on an all-star team at the end of the sixth-grade season, the last season for Little League football before kids are eligible to play middle school sports in Texas. Interested in music, he also began taking guitar lessons and quickly was playing his favorite Metallica music.

Seventh Grade: Family and Work Take Hits

In his seventh-grade year, school continued to be a highlight for Chris. His poetry and drawings were published in the school's literary magazine, and one of his illustrations was chosen for the booklet's front cover. He played seventh grade football and made good grades. Despite the positives coming from school and sports, at home we began to see a contrary attitude from Chris now and then. But his achievements were honorable and special to us as parents. I still feel a sense of pride in Chris for all the gifts he had and his ability to set, focus on, and accomplish goals.

Early in the spring semester of his seventh-grade year, we began receiving family counseling from a licensed professional counselor, primarily because of growing hostility among the three of us. We were facing fairly common issues experienced by many families in our stage of life—evolving midlife personal and career goals, financial stress of a child in college coupled with a sense of loss anticipating an empty nest, and elderly parents needing more from us in a reversal of roles. We found ourselves barking, snapping, and yelling at each other much of the time. A lot of blame was being passed around, and anger was becoming a constant, unwanted visitor in our family. A lot of the counseling centered on managing our stress, improving our communication and problem-solving skills, involving Chris in family decision making, and identifying and setting new rules and expectations appropriate for Chris's growing maturity. Our first session of family counseling marked the beginning of our roller-coaster ride. However, we did not know we had tickets when we first climbed aboard.

One thing we learned in counseling was that Rob and I had our own conflicts that were separate from any parenting issues with Chris. We knew Chris's issues—more opposition and less cooperation with the family, more secretiveness and less conversation about his life at school and with friends, more temper outbursts and less problem solving with us, and more taking off on his own and less asking permission.

The counselor had a specialization in art therapy, which was one of the reasons I chose him to work with Chris. Chris was very creative in several areas—music, art, writing, and, as we later learned, inventive deviousness. Chris did benefit from the counseling sessions because he was angry about all the stress in our family. The art therapy sessions provided him with a hands-on emotional outlet in a mode he understood and with a therapist who helped him identify the range and intensity of his feelings. Rob and I benefited because we were forced to discuss long-ignored differences that had begun to rub raw places in our relationship. On Saturday mornings while Chris slept in, Rob and I spent hours talking through the sore spots at any voice level we needed. For nine months the counseling created a short pause at the beginning of our roller-coaster ride. I think God gave us a blessing of time that allowed Rob and me to renew ourselves as partners for our unknown struggles ahead. And Chris received his first training in a valuable coping strategy to deal with his own stress and a Band-Aid that temporarily covered his early symptoms of bipolar disorder.

During the summer following seventh grade, we continued to take Chris for counseling with the art therapist in order to keep a handle on some of the acting-out behavior he occasionally displayed. This was as much for Rob and me as it was for Chris. We all benefited from being accountable to the counselor for improving our communication skills and parenting strategies.

There was another reason Rob and I stayed in counseling. In May, Rob's company had downsized, and he found himself unemployed. Downsizing is a euphemism for letting people go, reducing forces, eliminating positions, firing staff, and determining that services are no longer needed. That was a major blow to the whole family, but the blow to Rob's self-confidence was immense. He was forty-eight years old, and the economy was not in a happy place for the unemployed. The event was totally unexpected. He was notified midday, was not allowed to return to his office, and was escorted out by security. Company protocol made him feel like a criminal. The world did not seem to be the same place it had been the day before. Both of us were whirling in total shock.

Thankfully, our coming together to support Chris with more effective parenting strategies and communication skills had already strengthened our marital relationship. We brainstormed and problem solved and took steps to secure us financially and maintain Will's college goal to graduate from the University of Texas at Austin, which was also our alma mater.

> It was easy to become gripped with fear and to despair over our future. . . . Shame began to creep into our souls.

We endured some pretty sharp curves on the roller coaster. It was easy to become gripped with fear and to despair over our future. Rob and I had to work at keeping each other feeling upbeat and hopeful. Shame began to creep into our souls. Rob especially felt as if he had failed his family. I grieved for him. I wanted to make everything right. I commanded myself to stay cheerful, keep life going, stay on track—act okay and everything will be okay. We did not know that this was the beginning of our first big pileup of stress.

Shortly after Rob lost his job, our counselor shared his concern that Chris may have begun experimenting with drugs, probably marijuana. He advised us to take Chris for a drug test. We made a plan with our family doctor and took Chris in for a "routine" checkup. We did not go into the examining room, trusting our doctor to confront this issue with Chris. He did, and Chris cooperated openly. The doctor ordered a drug test, and it later came back positive, which Chris had already admitted it would. Rob and I were calm when we joined the doctor and Chris in the examination room. Our improved communication and parenting skills and our planning ahead with two trusted professionals helped Chris see our love and concern for him, and he accepted the consequences of his actions—limited summer activities, closer monitoring from us, and greater expectations for respectfulness, cooperation, and responsibility around the house.

The summer went smoothly. Rob took on some carpentry jobs, an avocation for him before his corporate job loss, and involved Chris with him daily. Like father, like son. They both prospered spiritually, mentally, and physically. It was artistic and body-exhausting work, for which they were paid. No shame there. Because of their long hours away from home and my being on summer break from my school counseling job, I started a successful weight-loss and exercise program. Will had a good summer adventure, too, selling books in Tennessee as part of a college work group. It was a win-win for all of us, reminding me that God's blessings come in unexpected ways.

Eighth Grade: Sharp Curves and Upside Down

We were all eager to start the new school year in August. We each launched off on our own, and thinking all was well, we terminated the counseling. We felt healthy and were enjoying our positive relationships within the family. Rob had made new career goals and was focused on a new start. I always got excited at the beginning of school. I loved my job as an elementary school counselor and adored my colleagues, but I especially looked forward to seeing the children again. I was always amazed at the growth and change that happened over summer break. Will was back from Tennessee with money in his pocket and looking forward to his sophomore year at the University of Texas in Austin. Chris was also excited about starting his last year in middle school and seemed to be in a good place mentally and emotionally. I'm sure Chris was experiencing that feeling of being BMOC—big man on campus—as he began the eighth grade. And probably, like most other eighth graders, he worked at making it more challenging for us and his teachers to guide him through a significant life passage. The "senioritis" that afflicted Chris did not show up immediately. During the fall semester Chris remained in advanced classes, played middle school football, and continued his guitar lessons. Little did Rob and I know that Chris began living a secret life shortly after the start of eighth grade. Evidence of his poor choices did not show up until months later. Evidence of my denial became apparent about the same time.

Early in the spring semester of eighth grade, Chris's grades began to fall. I thought he was involved in too many activities, but he loved them all and didn't want to change anything. Shortly after report cards came out, I received a call from one of his teachers telling me Chris was having trouble staying awake in class. I was still not too worried, thinking he was so busy. Course work was more demanding, and he was developing a social life with a cute girlfriend who was also in the eighth grade. I told his teacher that Chris promised to bring up his grades the next six weeks' grading period and that I would make sure he was in bed at a reasonable hour.

Soon we began to see evidence of some lies. Rob encountered Chris in the midst of a nighttime attack of vomiting. Chris told his dad that he felt as if he was getting the flu. One night our neighbor called the police in the wee morning hours because he saw a prowler on the roof of our garage. He came over and woke us up so we wouldn't be alarmed when the police car arrived. Next we received a second call from Chris's teacher reporting that he was now coming in late to class after lunch or was not returning at all. This class period was split at the lunchtime for Chris's grade level. Basically, Chris would attend the first half of class, go to lunch, and then give himself three choices for the second half of class—return on time, return late, or not return at all. After all, official attendance was taken at the beginning of class. Following this second call from Chris's teacher, red flags not only waved in front of our eyes but also began hitting us in the face. My professional training kicked in. Chris's falling grades, sleeping in class, unexplained absences, and history with drug use were all potential

My professional training kicked in. Chris's failing grades, sleeping in class, unexplained absences, and history with drug use were all potential indicators that my son was in trouble and that this was more than adolescent growing pains.

indicators that my son was in trouble and that this was more than adolescent growing pains.

It was now clear to us that others who knew Chris were becoming increasingly concerned about his behavior. Rob and I reflected on the episode of vomiting, the neighbor's report of a prowler on our garage roof, and the calls from Chris's teacher. Alternative explanations for these events quickly came to mind:

- He was very drunk that night when he got sick and vomited.
- He was sneaking in and out of his upstairs' bedroom at night, passing across the roof from a breezeway to the garage, then making a short drop to the ground.
- He was skipping lunch to get high with friends.

Chris had been flying over the roller-coaster tracks, but now the three of us were upside down on the first loop. How had the ride changed so quickly from the hopefulness of last summer?

A Diagnosis and First Manic Episode

Chris's deteriorating behavior—his growing sullenness, acting out, and loss of interest in school—coupled with our family history of bipolar disorder in close relatives, led me to make an appointment with a child-and-adolescent psychiatrist. The doctor took a complete family history, conducted family and individual interviews, and ordered medical tests for Chris, including a sleep-deprived EEG. The purpose of this test was to rule out a seizure disorder or other brain complication from an earlier concussion Chris had suffered. To complete this medical test, Rob and I had to keep Chris awake for a full twenty-four-hour day and then take him in for the EEG. We took turns with this parenting duty. The test was negative for any brain injuries or disorders. With physiological medical conditions ruled out, the psychiatrist diagnosed

Chris with bipolar disorder, and medication was prescribed. Chris was initially treated with an antidepressant and later a combination of antidepressants, mood stabilizers, and an atypical antipsychotic. We agreed to bring him in for monthly follow-up appointments with the psychiatrist and regular urine drug tests.

The last month of eighth grade was rocky for all of us. Chris's grades did not improve, but he was admitted to the National Junior Honor Society based on his excellent performance in the sixth grade through the fall semester of eighth grade. Talk about paradoxical feelings! Should we feel proud or ashamed? We chose not to attend the induction ceremony. Then we had a major confrontation with Chris over his not meeting a family rule. He was expected to cooperate at home, be mannerly, and complete his schoolwork. The positive consequence for keeping his end of the bargain was that he would be allowed to attend the eighth grade end-of-year party in the neighborhood. The reward for his maintaining respectful behavior was strong but not strong enough. He basically blew off school and any semblance of cooperation at home. When he was told he could not go to the party, he ran off and attended anyway. Rob and I anticipated what he would do and waited for him outside the party when everyone was leaving. He saw us in our vehicle and started running again. We followed along beside him until he got too tired to run anymore. He got in the truck, and we all drove home. Rob and I felt somewhat smug with this uneventful capture of our son. Privately we both empathized with his position, missing out on this special ending event of middle school, but we held our ground when we got home and told Chris to go to bed; we would discuss the matter in the morning.

> Chris was nowhere to be found. He had run away again. We felt angry with ourselves and ashamed of our short-sightedness and were scared at this turn of events.

When Rob and I awoke the next day, Chris was nowhere to be found. He had run away again during the night. We felt angry with ourselves and ashamed of our shortsightedness and were scared at this turn of events. It was four days before we located him through friends. He came home. We called the psychiatrist and took him in for an appointment the following day. The doctor made some adjustments in Chris's medication, and we restarted the counseling with the art therapist. We had a treatment plan in place, and it gave us a focus for the summer leading into high school.

Having this professional support network, Rob and I did not feel so alone in dealing with Chris's increasingly nasty attitude. For the most part, we maintained our cool and our sanity. From Chris's point of view, his manipulation and button pushing in order to create a chaotic household was having less success. But the coming summer did not stand a chance of reaching that feeling of hopefulness we experienced the previous summer. Instead, it apparently presented the ultimate challenge for a teenage male in a budding manic state.

We knew our problem was escalating. This pre–high school summer was looking long. Rob and I focused even more closely on picking our battles, staying calm, and setting limits that were reasonable for a fifteen-year-old. Will stayed in Austin that summer, so it was only the three of us dealing with our turmoil. Chris cooperated just enough with the limits we set for our family to make it through the summer without experiencing a dangerous explosion. However, his behavior became increasingly strange over the summer, and it was just the beginning.

Almost immediately Chris's oppositional behavior escalated. For one of the urine tests, he fried bacon for his breakfast and poured the bacon grease in the specimen jar on the day of our scheduled visit to the psychiatrist. He placed the jar in a small brown-paper bag, neatly folded on top, and set it on the counter. When I came into the kitchen that morning, I was pleased to see how responsibly he was acting. We took the little bag along on our visit and handed it over to the psychiatrist's nurse. She packaged it for the lab and sent it off. I don't know how Chris was able to sit through that appointment without laughing his head off at the psychiatrist and me. Later the psychiatrist told me wryly that we should consider this a positive test.

Chris stayed on a cooking binge following the bacon episode. Garlic became his food of choice. I would wake up in the middle of the night smelling garlic. When I got up and went into the kitchen, Chris would be cooking something on the stove. He used huge amounts of garlic and said he liked it that way. The house would smell like garlic for days. I'm still not sure why he did this. Did he like the smell? Did he like the flavor? Did garlic in excessive amounts create some kind of high for him? Did it cover up another strong smell he wanted to hide?

Over the next few months, Chris started putting safety pins in his T-shirts when he wore them—lots of pins, as if they were a kind of embellishment. He started piercing his ears and tongue. At one point he had nine piercings in one earlobe. When I discovered the tongue piercing, I was horrified. Chris was still in braces at age fifteen, so I called his orthodontist before our next appointment and asked him to talk to Chris about this. He told Chris how to keep it clean and uninfected! I was shocked. I expected him to tell Chris that he had to remove the tongue piercing.

Chris's strange behavior was not limited to this pre–high school summer. His next experimentation came during high school when he began putting self-made tattoos on his body. He became enamored with Wicca and tarot cards. He put huge chains on his wallet and wore them around his neck. He began to dress in only black clothing. At various times he grew his hair long, bleached it a garish yellow, dyed it hot pink, and shaved his head. What did these things mean to him? What was he thinking? Where was he headed in his life? Everything Chris did seemed extreme. These behaviors crept up on us one at a time; then we would be slapped in the face with an outburst that we never dreamed we would see in one of our children. Before we got a grip on one new behavior, the next one would pop up. Another bizarre and prophetic mode of dress also started up in high school. Chris began wearing a fuzzy knit ski cap almost all the time, year-round, in the house and outside, even in Houston's ninety-five-degree summers. Later as his illness became much more severe, Chris explained to me that the fuzzy hat helped keep out telepathic brain waves that were directed at him from the television, radio, and people near him. He included Rob and me in this group of *telepaths*, his word for those he believed were entering and programming his mind. Looking back, I think Chris's first manic episode in eighth grade—the running away coupled with drug use—pushed his brain off track just as he was beginning to establish an adult persona and belief system.

Rob and I stayed with our plan during the summer before high school, taking Chris to biweekly appointments with the therapist and monthly appointments with the psychiatrist for medication checks and urine tests. Our guilt and shame were growing as we kept asking ourselves what we had done so wrong in rearing this child. It was a struggle for Rob and me to keep putting one foot in front of the other. Much of the time we felt exhausted and afraid that Chris's mania had much more in store for us. By the end of the summer, the bipolar diagnosis seemed right on.

5

High School Hell: Ninth Grade

After a rough summer closely supervising Chris, Rob and I were both glad for school to start. While we looked forward to Chris being at school during the day, we had no rosy expectations about how the year might proceed. At the first of September, I located the Palmer Drug Abuse Program (PDAP), a drug abuse twelve-step group that was designed for both teens and their parents. PDAP is still active in Houston. Chris totally rejected this option, but Rob and I and our professional support team were 100 percent in favor. We started immediately after I made the first contact with the organization to learn times and locations of meetings.

Taking this step was scary for me as I had never personally known anyone in a twelve-step program. No one in my immediate family or circle of friends had a problem with alcohol or drugs. In fact, Rob and I rarely drank any alcoholic beverages and rarely kept it in the house. We had never experimented with drugs of any kind. Alcohol was typically a special-event beverage for us, usually enjoyed in dinners out with friends and family.

In September, Rob also began teaching college night classes as an adjunct economics professor. For this reason, and in spite of his objection, Chris and I attended the first PDAP session on our own. I was worried about Chris's willingness to cooperate without his father along. However, Chris went along with the plan, and when we arrived, Chris went into a youth group, and I went into a parent group. I did not know the protocol—first names only and the reading of the twelve steps to start the group out for the evening. When it came my turn to read a step, I burst into tears. Still determined to do my part, I blubbered through. The rest of the group let me blubber, and the circle reading process continued until all twelve steps were read. The facilitator threw out a topic for discussion, and individuals shared. I do not remember another detail of that meeting—just that I survived it. The three of us continued in PDAP for most of Chris's high school years. Rob and I became involved in helping out wherever needed. I encountered many other parents who, like me, felt so lost on their first night in the group. PDAP was a tremendous help to us as parents. It was educational and supportive, and it created a network of others walking in our shoes. Having a teen who is abusing drugs brings lots of baggage to a family. But the now-troubled young person was also once a baby, tiny and helpless and totally dependent on the adult to provide safety as he grew to maturity. There is no script to guide a parent when drug use rears its ugly head in his or her child's path. Rob and I did what we were confident was best, and we did it diligently. Despite the destination our path ultimately led us to, I am proud of our involvement in PDAP. It is likely that it saved our son from teenage death by suicide, risky behavior, or a drug overdose. It did save my sanity and strengthened my relationship with my husband.

There is no script to guide a parent when drug use rears its ugly head in your child's path.

Another benefit for me from my participation in PDAP was that I grew professionally because of the training I received and the networking I did with other parents living through the same ordeal. We all saw drug addiction up close and personal. At one time or another, every member of my support group felt as if we were literally in a war to protect the life and soul of a child. My empathy for parents who came to me as a school counselor was genuine, and the knowledge I shared with them was practical and doable. My counselor colleagues often sought me out for consultation and tips on community resources. I organized parenting programs in my school district that annually provided support for hundreds of parents. I headed up this program for fifteen years, until I retired in 2008. The programs are still taught by school counselors in my district and offer inexpensive benefits for parents at all grade levels.

As a family, the three of us went to PDAP three times a week all through Chris's ninth grade year. We also kept taking Chris to the psychiatrist, who worked closely with us monitoring and adjusting his medication for the bipolar disorder. We stopped the counseling with the art therapist because of all the group and family sessions we went to at PDAP. For Chris, the program offered substance-abuse education, prevention, accountability, and a social group of nonusing teens. For Rob and me, it provided education on addiction behaviors, empathy and support from other parents, and specific strategies to use when faced with a crisis.

Another important step I took early in Chris's ninth grade year was to request that the school evaluate him for special education services. Though time-intensive, the process was relatively easy, especially given the evidence of his downward spiral over a one-and-a-half-year period from all advanced classes to mostly failing grades in regular classes. The fact that he was already diagnosed with bipolar disorder meant that the psychiatrist simply had to provide a summary of treatment and diagnosis to add to the school district's educational testing. The completed report clearly showed that Chris was performing academically below his intellectual potential, far below. Special education support in Texas is not meant to help a student move from B's to A's or from regular classes to advanced classes. These services provide an eligible student with an individual education plan (IEP). The goal of Chris's IEP was to enable him to function on grade level. Chris was in ninth grade. He needed to pass ninth-grade course work and be able to move on to the tenth grade at the end of the year. Chris's disability was identified as serious emotional disturbance (SED). The school's evaluation, including the psychiatric summary and diagnosis, allowed Chris to receive interventions designed to lessen the stress level endemic to a four-thousand-student suburban high school. Chris, the school, and I all knew that Chris could learn, but only if he was mentally, emotionally, and behaviorally stable. The ups and downs of his mood swings interfered with Chris's ability to learn. Medication was not able to stabilize him enough to foster learning. He needed smaller classes, specially trained teachers, and close monitoring of his academic progress. There was also a behavioral component to his IEP. Educators who teach students with an emotional disability take many extra classes and workshops to become highly skilled in effective behavior management. They often hold advanced degrees and have a heart for working with at-risk students. They are trained in recognizing the signs of escalating stress and triggers of acting-out behavior. Having a calm voice, using nonthreatening body language, and giving a student space and a moment to regain self-control were all part of the skills that made Chris's classroom a place of learning rather than a hostile work environment. Chris was taught to use cooling-off periods to manage his feelings, which was reminiscent of his first counseling sessions in seventh grade. Helping a student talk through a problem rather than acting out in anger was an important skill that was second nature to his teachers. Chris and these teachers formed wonderful relationships, and he made academic progress.

More Stress and Now Grief

Behavioral decisions Chris made outside his classroom, however, were less positive. Late in November, Chris bought LSD in the high school parking lot and was found under the influence of the drug by school personnel. He was given three days' out-of-school suspension and then was placed at the district's alternative disciplinary campus for six weeks. In Chris's third week at the alternative campus, my mother was hospitalized with a sudden illness and was in ICU for five days. She died on December 16, two weeks after Chris's fifteenth birthday. Two days later Chris and Will were pallbearers at her funeral.

My mother's unexpected death was a great loss for me. She had recently signed a contract to sell her house and was planning to move in with us. She, Rob, and I had held a big garage sale the weekend before she became ill. I took her to the hospital on Monday morning because she was having trouble breathing. On Friday night she died. As her power of attorney, my brother went to the closing on her house on Thursday. In between my trips to visit her at the hospital, I met with the house inspector, packed boxes, got ready for the movers on Friday, and cleaned her house for the new owners. On Saturday morning I shopped for a pretty gown for her burial and met my brother at the funeral home to make arrangements.

In addition to planning a funeral and thinking of Christmas just around the corner, Rob and I were loaded with other responsibilities in our jobs common to this time of year. He had final exams to administer and grade for the five courses he taught and end-of-semester reports to submit. I had heavy end-of-semester responsibilities at my school. Will was home from college for his holiday break. He signed up to take a minicourse at a local college; no winter ski vacation was in sight for him. Chris finished his suspension at the alternative campus. Our family was beyond stressed. We prayed for God's strength and kept moving forward one step at a time.

Stress turned out to be Chris's worst enemy. It seemed to trigger episodes that pushed him into either depression or mania. Rob and I recognized the signs of a mood swing, and at times Chris did as well.

Stress turned out to be Chris's worst enemy. It seemed to trigger episodes that pushed him into either depression or mania. Rob and I recognized the signs of a mood swing and, at times, Chris did as well. He would make decisions on his own to increase, decrease, or stop taking his medication. Such a pattern can be disastrous behaviorally, emotionally, and physically. Being an invincible teenager, at least in his mind, Chris sometimes took his own version of medication—marijuana, alcohol, amphetamines, LSD, and inhalants. This had the effect of throwing gasoline on a raging fire.

First Psychiatric Hospital—Suicidal Ideation, Overdose, and More

Chris's first expression of suicidal ideation was made to his PDAP counselor in late January. By this time he was facing another big adjustment since he had returned to his regular high school from the alternative campus. With the counselor's support he told us about his feelings of depression and anxiety. He had begun to cut his arms with razor blades and other sharp instruments. Shortly after this counseling session, he took an overdose of his prescription antidepressant, Zoloft. The effect of the Zoloft overdose caused Chris to become extremely aggressive toward me, laughing, jumping around, pushing, and threatening like a crazy person. Because his behavior was so strange and hostile, I decided to count the pills in the prescription bottle and found that many were missing. I called the psychiatrist and scheduled an immediate appointment. Chris refused to go with me and stood screaming at me in the front yard as I drove off without him. Shortly after, Chris was admitted to a psychiatric hospital due to his deteriorating mental state. His diagnosis was bipolar disorder, depression, and polysubstance abuse. He was discharged following twenty-three days of treatment. He was medically stabilized from the overdose, and new medications were gradually introduced.

The effect of the Zoloft overdose caused Chris to become extremely aggressive toward me, laughing, jumping around, pushing, and threatening like a crazy person.

While hospitalized, Chris participated in group and individual therapy. Rob and I attended family counseling sessions. The best outcome from this first of Chris's many hospitalizations was meeting the licensed professional counselor who became Chris's therapist and our lifeline to sanity for the next ten years.

Our bonding with the therapist came quickly as Chris had five more serious incidents before the end of ninth grade. Chris was discharged from this first hospital stay in March, and two weeks later he ran away from home. He was gone for three days. He came home primarily because the sudden withdrawal from taking his prescribed medication, Effexor, was making him sick with flulike symptoms. In April, Chris overdosed on Ecstasy, and we took him to the emergency room. He was hospitalized overnight in a medical hospital, where his condition stabilized, and it was discovered that he had a heart murmur. While recovering during that brief stay, Chris stole a sterile syringe and needles from a nurse's cart parked in the hallway near his room.

We did not know Chris had taken the items from the nurse's cart at the hospital until one week later. While listening in on a Friday night telephone call between Chris and a PDAP friend, I heard the friend screaming, "No, no, Chris! Stop, stop!" I yelled at Rob immediately to run upstairs and check on Chris. He found Chris holding the syringe and beginning to stick it into his arm. We had noticed that Chris's forearms had looked red and swollen the past few days. When we had asked him about it, he told us that he had done too many push-ups and his arms were sore. How naive we were! His answer did not make sense, but we took what he said at face value. His school friends had known for a full week that Chris had injected Mini Thins, an over-the-counter ephedrine preparation sold in gas station convenience stores.

Just before Rob entered his room, Chris had diluted the pills in a liquid and was ready to inject the drug solution for a second time that week. Rob stopped him. I called the Poison Control Center. They had never heard of Mini Thins and advised me to call 911. Instead, we bundled Chris into the car and drove to the hospital emergency room.

The outcome of injecting a nonsterile liquid into his body was that he developed severe internal abscesses in both arms at the injection site. Fortunately, he injected into the muscle and missed hitting a vein. Another blessing! But after twenty-four hours on intravenous antibiotics in the ER, the infection continued to worsen. Chris's arms were as red and hot as fire. Late the second night Chris had emergency surgery on both arms and was in danger of having his arms amputated at the elbow. The surgery to clean and drain the abscesses was successful. Chris remained hospitalized in a sterile, no-visitor environment for twelve days and then was transferred to the psychiatric hospital for a fifteen-day period. He stabilized again on medication, and "chronic mental illness" was added to his multiaxial diagnosis. He still had bandages on his arms when he was discharged from the psychiatric hospital in early May. After coming home, Rob changed Chris's bandages daily until he was completely released by the surgeon.

It was the orthopedic surgeon who educated us that drug abuse not only can result in death by overdose, but it can also result in life as a double amputee. I continue to thank God for this man's skill and compassion. I thank PDAP for teaching me that it was okay to listen in on my son's phone conversations when he was living an addictive lifestyle as a minor in my home. I am thankful for his PDAP friend who screamed at him to stop. I never again trusted his school friends who had known that what Chris was doing was dangerous and stupid and had kept it to themselves.

Chris did not stop the manic, addictive behaviors even after his arm surgery and psychiatric hospital stay. While attending a PDAP retreat in a small Texas country town a few days after his discharge from the psychiatric hospital, Chris overdosed on two prescription medications, Tegretol and Risperdal. We received a phone call and were told that Chris had suddenly become unable to speak clearly or stand up. He was taken to a local hospital for examination, and blood work had been sent to a lab. Of course, no one thought to run tests for the presence of excessive amounts of his antipsychotic and mood stabilizer meds. We drove the two hundred miles at high speed and made the trip in a little over two hours. When we arrived, Chris was better. We took him home, feeling relieved that he was okay. While Rob drove, Chris told us what he had done.

Summer: Making Up for Lost Time

Five months of ninth grade had passed with Chris in an uncontrolled manic state. Clearly, he received no education that spring semester. Consequently because of his eligibility for special education support, Chris was enrolled in a highly structured day hospital program from mid-May through the end of July. He attended five days a week for two and a half months. Chris made up the missed course work and participated in group and individual counseling sessions. The psychiatrist again changed his medication. All three of us regularly attended PDAP that summer. Rob and I helped sponsor PDAP's weekend fun activities and got to know many parents and teens well. The limited freedom, consistent routine, stable environment, and medication change helped Chris's mood become stable. He earned his thirty-day sobriety chip and associated only with friends who were in PDAP with him. He did not act manic this summer.

Another family event happened that summer that saddened us all. Rob's mother was diagnosed with cancer in mid-June. It turned out to be untreatable. She would live only five more months after suffering a stroke following her cancer surgery. Thankfully, God keeps to Himself the exact moment of a person's death, and we remained hopeful that Rob's mother would recover.

As the summer stretched into late August, Rob and I wondered what tenth grade would bring, fearing what Chris had in store for us. This summer was not as good as two summers before, but it was better than the last summer with Chris.

6

High School Hell Moderates: Tenth Grade

My simple description of bipolar disorder is "erratic, unpredictable, and deceptive behavior." Just when we thought progress was finally being made, a crisis would engulf us. Our times were rocky all throughout Chris's high school years. The roller coaster swung wide, teetering on two wheels many times, slinging us so hard we thought the safety bar was undone. But after a while it became apparent that our family schedule of Rob's teaching at night and my working during the day was a blessing. One of us was always with Chris.

Rather than allow Chris to ride the school bus in tenth grade, Rob started taking him to school at 7:00 every morning and picking him up at 2:30 every afternoon. Chris continued in the smaller adaptive behavior (AB) classes. The mood swings stood in abeyance for the most part, and Chris made good academic progress during the fall semester. Rob would be the one to go to school and pick Chris up if something happened. Out-of-school suspension was an occasional consequence for Chris because of some kind of behavioral outburst. Rob would have a short conference with the teacher, counselor, or assistant principal, collect Chris and his schoolwork, sign him out of school, and take him home. They would talk about what had happened, and he would get Chris started on whatever schoolwork he was missing. Rob would then call me at work to tell me about the incident and what limits and agreements he and Chris had made. I would follow through with the plan when I got home. Often Chris would want to talk to me about his feelings and behavior. He knew how damaging the outbursts were. He scared himself. We would review his strategies, and we usually had a quiet evening at home or would attend a PDAP meeting. The next day Rob would have to go into the school office to check Chris back into school after the suspension. Rob was so much more than Mr. Mom. I'm sure he never expected to play such an important role in his younger son's life, but he did it sacrificially with love.

Another Great Loss

Another disturbing event happened in October. Rob's mother was now receiving hospice care at home, and Rob's dad was her primary care giver. They lived in a nearby small town north of Houston, and we would visit most weekends when possible. During one visit Chris stole some of his grandmother's pain medications: morphine and hydrocodone. He took excessive amounts of these drugs while at school but was not noticed to be under the influence by school personnel. Neither his therapist nor his psychiatrist understood how Chris's system could have metabolized these drugs without his becoming very ill. We learned about it when a school friend called to tell us what Chris had done. Again, this kind of news was hardly believable. Our sense of reality had a hard time taking in Chris's behavior. She was his Grannie, who loved him dearly, who roasted marshmallows with him in the fire pit in the country, taught him how to make pudding in the blender, and gave him art lessons. Before confronting Chris, Rob called his dad and asked him to count the pills in the prescription bottles. A large number were missing. We told Chris what we had learned, and he admitted what he had done. As far as I know, he always told us the truth when confronted if he was in a calm emotional state. He definitely lied when he was manic but did not when we were talking to the real Chris. He felt ashamed of what he had done.

Rob's mother died on November 30. On Thanksgiving I'd taken our dinner to Grannie's house so we could all be with her and Grandpa. She was not able to be at the table with us, but she knew we were there. That was the last time we saw her. Just a few days later she died in her sleep. Like my mother's death the year before, her death and funeral were wedged in with Thanksgiving, Will's and Chris's birthdays, and Christmas. Rob, his dad, brother, and sister took care of his mother's funeral arrangements. Again Will and Chris were pallbearers. My mother-in-law was incredibly special to me. She was a wise, caring woman, and she loved her grandsons unconditionally. Our mothers died within eleven months of each other. This was a great loss.

The rest of Chris's tenth grade year was rather uneventful, a blessing we all desperately needed. The strangest thing about that school year was that Chris stopped seeing his psychiatrist late in the fall semester and was not taking any meds during the spring semester. He had special education support at school and regularly saw his therapist. I think the real glue that held Chris together that year was Rob.

Life goes on, as did the roller-coaster ride of Chris's mental illness.

Rob and I came to realize that our family was dealing with a seriously chronically ill child, along with all the other stressful events that families face. Life goes on, as did the roller-coaster ride of Chris's mental illness. Financial issues continued to challenge us. Rob took on extra classes. I worked during the summer at a local community college and taught parenting classes at night during the school year. Will worked throughout his college time at UT, applied for loans, and served as treasurer of a fraternity, which provided him with a free room in the frat house.

The New Year, 1997, brought a sense of calm for us, and we were thankful for it. We encountered no big loops or wheels off the track until December, when the glue holding Chris together let go.

7

Minuses and Pluses: Eleventh Grade

Chris started eleventh grade still in adaptive behavior classes. He was sixteen and had gotten a job over the summer. He continued working part-time after school and added a work co-op program to his schedule. This meant that he got out of school at 1:00 p.m. instead of 2:30 each day. He had a school supervisor as well as a work supervisor and was accountable to both of them. All went well at first, but eventually Chris's grades in his academic classes began to suffer. It was easy to see that Chris was becoming more and more stressed with his combined work and school schedule. He had been successful in both areas for more than six months, but now irritability and a depressed mood became apparent. Our goal was to get him through Christmas, which was a busy season on his job, and then just do school in the spring. He was still not seeing a psychiatrist, nor was he taking medication. The school special education team had become a strong support for him.

Final exams approached in mid-December, and Chris needed to ace them in order to bring up his low grades to a solid passing average. Life goes on, as we knew it did, and unexpected things sometimes happened that caused problems not connected to our roller-coaster ride. One of these events happened the night before Chris's final exam. His girlfriend, the cute one from eighth grade, was in a serious car accident. Of course, all of us were worried about her, and it was a late night in our household. Her injuries turned out to be minor, but the friend who was riding with her sustained a head injury, and her condition was serious. Fatigue, the stress of a final exam, and worry about his girlfriend were all in Chris's mind when he rushed through the school doors in the morning, trying to beat the tardy bell.

Remember the fuzzy knit ski caps he liked to wear? He was wearing one that morning. It was December and cold outside. An assistant principal approached Chris almost immediately when he entered the school building, pointed at the cap, and gestured for him to take it off. Whether he also told Chris to remove the hat or just motioned with his hand, I don't know. Chris thought he was going to pull the cap off of his head and shoved the AP's hand away. The AP shoved Chris up against a wall, and all hell broke loose.

The chaos created by that event lasted through the Christmas holidays into the start of the spring semester. Chris was suspended until the matter could be resolved. The school wanted to expel him, which is the absolute worst consequence that can be levied educationally. We had several conferences with the school that involved both the high school administration and the special education staff. We ultimately made a formal appeal to the district-level administration and finally agreed on a plan that was acceptable to both parties. The fact was, Chris had an Individual Education Plan for behavior that listed steps to be followed when he was in a potentially volatile situation, which this had been. The AP should have known who Chris was, specifically because he was a student with a special education label of Serious Emotional Disturbance in the AP's high school. Fortunately for school personnel, there were few of those students in even a large high school. It was the most severe label under special-ed guidelines. People who work with individuals who are mentally ill ("emotionally disturbed" in school jargon) know to give personal space, speak calmly, display nonthreatening body language, and allow for the situation to diffuse before taking action. This is common training provided to medical personnel, police officers, emergency medical services (EMS) personnel, criminal justice officers, mental health workers, and school personnel (especially administrators).

Chris should not have shoved the AP's hand. The AP should not have shoved Chris against the wall, resulting in a greater escalation. Wrong, wrong, wrong for both parties. But to permanently kick our son out of school was something Rob and I could not let happen. We knew much more about bipolar disorder than the school did. We lived with it every day. On the day of the hat incident, Chris was wound as tight as a spring because of fatigue, stress, and worry.

Severe mental illness is like any other serious, potentially fatal disease and is not usually considered curable.

The school psychologist wanted to say that the stressful event had happened the night before, and Chris should have known to respect the AP the next morning. Again, wrong, wrong, wrong. Chris's reaction was defensive. He was already fighting to keep himself under control in the face of enough stress to send him over the edge. The school psychologist wanted to divide Chris's mental illness into OFF and ON positions on a dial. It doesn't work that way. Severe mental illness is like any other serious, potentially fatal disease and is not usually considered curable. Most often it is manageable over a person's lifetime with proper treatment. But it can dramatically erupt if the perfect storm of negative events occurs in a person's life. In Chris's case we knew the disease was always present—alternately existing in a kind of calm remission, a determinedly suicidal depression, or a flagrantly out-of-control mania. The switch was always in the ON position, but at times his illness was in sleep mode. All this came too fast for us. My life felt totally out of control.

Spring Semester—High School Recovery

The plan we followed after the Special Education Manifestation of Dangerousness meeting, which basically concluded that Chris was too dangerous to remain in school, was to assign him to a permanent, all-day cooperative work program. He was out of school but not suspended or expelled. He could not be on campus for any reason. In the meantime I applied to enroll Chris in an alternative academic high school program in the district where I worked.

This was a unique program for "different drummers." These were students that, because of unusual family circumstances, loss of credit, or a desire to graduate early from high school, did not fit well in a standard 7:30 to 2:30 high school program. The school's enrollment was purposefully kept low. The classes were small. Only dedicated teachers who were drawn to helping students at risk of not graduating from high school were hired to teach there. The school had block scheduling, which meant that every class met for two-hour periods. The school year was divided into four, nine-week semesters. Classes started at 8:00 a.m. and went until 8:00 p.m. Students could create their class schedules to work around family and employment needs as well as work toward personal goals. A schedule could be split with early and late classes, leaving the afternoon free for personal or job-related responsibilities. Community college classes were held in the same building, allowing students to take dual-credit courses. I knew this was where Chris needed to be.

My district was willing to take a chance on Chris. They knew his story, and he was on the outer edge of students that were usually accepted. We were allowed to submit an application for admission in March, prior to the start of the last quarter of the school year. The principal and counselor talked straight with Chris at our application interview. He had to agree to fulfill all the school's expectations. The school complied with all the usual Texas education laws regarding attendance, course requirements, and behavior.

One thing Chris had going for him was that he had already passed all state academic exams that were required for high school graduation in Texas. No matter his state of mind, those tests had always been easy for him, from elementary school on. His track record of success in the small adaptive behavior classes was also a factor that helped secure his admission. He and I were both anxious during that interview, but God had walked with us through those interview doors. Chris was admitted, and two short months later he had regained his credits for the second half of eleventh grade. In the fall he would be able to move on to the twelfth grade in that unique high school.

Will's college graduation coincided with this positive period in Chris's life. Attending his graduation ceremony in Austin following the successful completion of Chris's eleventh-grade year was a family affair, and we all were excited. Chris looked forward to his own high school graduation the coming year and expressed hope that he would be able to follow in Will's footsteps.

Will was a joy to us as parents during this period, although we rarely had time or energy to focus much attention on him. He understood our struggles with his six-year-younger brother. Will often called his dad in the mornings when Chris was at school and I was at work. They would talk about politics, the economy, financial issues, and world events—the topics Rob was teaching and Will was studying. I always heard about Rob's telephone conversations secondhand, but they were just as uplifting to me as they were to Chris. Will completed his bachelor's and master's degrees at UT in five years. He had a job lined up in Minnesota with a major agricultural products company before he graduated. Rob and I knew we would miss Will, but the successful launching of son number one filled us with hope for son number two.

8

A "Normal" Life: Twelfth Grade

Chris attended the alternative high school all of twelfth grade and graduated on time in May! Midyear he decided he wanted to start seeing a psychiatrist again and get back on medication. He was making mature choices to ensure his success at school. I also think part of the reason he made that decision was to protect me, because it was the district of my employment, and Chris did not want to bring shame on me. He also knew it was a privilege to be admitted to the school.

Chris was academically successful that year. He made friends and was liked by his teachers and administrators. He took part in special school projects. Chris had earned his driver's license during the summer and had gotten a job. Grandpa had given Grannie's car to Will after she died, so, in turn, Will passed down his older college car to Chris. Having a job and wheels of his own now, Chris was paying for his car insurance and gasoline. He continued to behave responsibly at home, school, and work.

Chris's only disciplinary infraction during the one and a half years he attended the alternative high school was smoking a cigarette in the school parking lot as he arrived at school one morning. For breaking that rule he was suspended from a day of school and was issued a ticket. He paid the ticket with his own money and apologized to the principal. For the first time since Chris was in seventh grade, our lives felt normal.

Dual Diagnosis

Bipolar disorder is a mental illness that is often linked with substance abuse. During two of Chris's years in his regular high school, mid-ninth grade to mid-eleventh grade, Chris's life was often out of control. His primary diagnoses from his psychiatrist were bipolar disorder, mixed, and polysubstance abuse disorder.

> Biplor disorder is a mental illness that is often linked with substance abuse . . . Chris chose to get high when he felt depressed and chose to get higher when he felt manic.

"Bipolar disorder, mixed" means that his mood swings came quickly, one after another. The diagnosis of polysubstance abuse disorder means that Chris chose to get high when he felt depressed and chose to get higher when he felt manic. One moment he was so depressed he talked of suicide. The next moment he was hostile and aggressive and refused to cooperate or show respect.

The medications prescribed by the psychiatrist were intended to level out the mood swings and prevent psychosis, but they never worked perfectly in Chris's case. They all had side effects that were at the least bothersome. Chris often felt groggy during the day. He would also have trouble going to sleep at night. He developed a tremor in his hands that affected his guitar playing, writing, and drawing. His mouth and lips always felt dry. One medication caused his hair to fall out. The meds themselves—the timing and dosages—were constantly being adjusted. Some required frequent lab tests to monitor safe blood levels.

The manic swings of bipolar disorder coupled with negative medication side effects often led Chris to be noncompliant with medication, a serious and ongoing problem. Our parent-supervision routine helped at home. Rob and I knew that a high stress level was a major mood-swing trigger for Chris, so we tried to monitor his stress level closely and see that he regularly took his meds. And his teachers did a great job during class time. Even though our roller-coaster ride felt imminently dangerous at times, attending Chris's high school graduation was incredibly fulfilling and joyful.

Part Three

PASSAGE TO YOUNG ADULTHOOD

9

Independence

Following his high school graduation in May, Chris decided to work and delay starting college for one year. Rob and I concurred. Chris was doing well on his job, working thirty-five to thirty-eight hours each week. He saved money and began contributing to a company-sponsored stock savings plan. He exhibited a calmness that we had not seen since sixth grade. He dressed nicely, kept regular hours, was liked and respected at work, and joined in with family activities. He got periodic raises and was asked to train new employees who were doing his same job.

Rob and I prospered during this period also. I left my elementary school position and was promoted to a central office administrative position in guidance and counseling. Rob had earned a positive reputation among the undergraduate students who signed up for his classes. He truly loved teaching economics and made his classes interesting. He always had been comfortable in giving public presentations, and his association with the teens in PDAP trained him to see life from the young adult's viewpoint. We could now depend on Rob's teaching as a year-round job, and with my raise and a longer contract, we were almost back to where we were when Rob left corporate life five years earlier. Chris was covering his own expenses, and Will had a good job in Minnesota.

After a full year of being out of school, Chris began taking courses at a local community college. He was successful that summer in taking twelve semester hours during the two terms. He registered again in the 2000 fall semester, taking typical freshman classes—English, algebra, history, and government. Since he was taking a full load of classes, in September Chris quit his job to focus on school. Again, Rob and I concurred. We did not want his stress level to increase so much that he began having trouble again, and a full course load was a lot to undertake, considering his up-and-down history in high school. Chris was still taking medication, seeing a psychiatrist, and going to counseling. His doctor prescribed Celexa to treat his depression, Lithobid for mood swings, Risperdal for his psychosis, and Adderall for attention deficit.

During the fall semester Chris was on the dean's list and was asked to join the National Honor Society for two-year colleges. We all were happy with life as it was and wanted to do what was necessary to ensure that it continued. We were in rebuilding mode and felt hopeful for the future.

But about halfway through the semester, Rob and I began to notice that Chris seemed to be withdrawing from us socially and was less communicative about how school was going. He began to perseverate on a research paper he was writing about Hitler and had difficulty completing other class assignments. He would stay up late at night working on the Hitler paper and then could not get up in time for a morning class. Rob and I saw the red flags again. By now it was near the Christmas holidays and the end of the semester. We just prayed that we would get through it soon, and then Chris would have a long break before the spring semester started. We looked forward to a fresh start for him in mid-January.

Whispers

One early December evening Chris was sitting in the dark in his bedroom. I stopped by to say hello, and we talked a minute. Chris told me in a soft voice, "I hear whispers." Not sure what he meant, I asked, "In your head?" He said yes and that it was like soft static but definitely in his head and not from inside his room or the yard outside. Neither of us knew what was causing this odd sensation he was having. I felt a grip of fear deep down but told him he probably had stopped-up ears. Chris had just turned twenty years old.

The end of the fall 2000 semester brought back memories of Chris's eighth grade spring semester in which he was inducted into the National Junior Honor Society while currently having all failing grades. He had been very successful with his first twelve semester hours in college but now was seemingly unable to complete his school assignments. The work he did on his Hitler research paper was way beyond the teacher's expectation and so comprehensive that his teacher allowed it to count for two papers. The original assignment in that history course was to write two papers on different topics, but Chris could not stop writing the first paper. It became an obsession for him, and it took him till the very end of the semester to complete it. Chris earned an A in that history class but then barely passed his other three courses.

> Psychosis was gaining on him again. The roller coaster was building speed rapidly.

Chris's "whispers" of two months before exploded into a manic, agitated psychotic state after Christmas. He had preregistered for spring classes but immediately dropped all except English, which later he also dropped. He was staying up late at night, going out with friends we did not know, and doing things we knew were not good for him. But Chris was twenty years old. Nothing he did merited the ringing of an alarm bell except to us as his parents. His behavior that spring began to match his ninth-grade year—loud, obnoxious, and often irritable. "Tough love" was a parenting approach advocated by some in a situation like ours. I was careful when sharing this period of turmoil with family or close friends, fearing I would be advised to kick him out of the house, pack a suitcase for him, leave it on the front porch, change the locks, and not let him come back home until he had a job.

But Rob and I knew we were dealing with an adult son who was seriously mentally ill and heading for a breakdown. Chris's behavior was not a result of a conduct disorder, rebelliousness, drug use, laziness, or being spoiled. He had gone through a calm, productive, and hopeful recovery period that had lasted almost three years, but it was now ending. Psychosis was gaining on him again. The roller coaster was rapidly building speed.

10

God, Telepathy, and the IRS

Early in the afternoon on Sunday, February 4, 2001, Chris threw us totally off balance when he announced that he wanted to be baptized at the evening church service. He had attended church regularly with us until life began to fall apart for him in eighth grade. At times when the roller coaster slowed a bit during his high school and college years, Chris would attend church with us, but he had not been in several months. After his announcement to us, he acted jittery the rest of the afternoon and was insistent about his decision. Rob talked to him at length and tried to understand what was really in his mind. Chris became more calm and continued to state that this was what he wanted to do, so Rob and I agreed to take him to church.

We sat on the back row, worried that Chris would bolt and run out. Energy and anxiety vibrated from his body. Likewise, every muscle in my body was tensed and ready to grab him if necessary. Rob sat on the other side of Chris and was feeling the same way. As the service ended, Chris responded to the invitation song and walked to the front of the auditorium where the minister was standing. At this point I wished we were sitting on the front row instead of the back row! Despite his extreme nervousness, Chris followed all the minister's instructions and was baptized.

Our faith in God's promise of an eternal life in heaven with Him does not remove our earthly trials. But He promises to go with us through our trials and provide us with His wisdom, comfort, and strength.

What mixed and confused feelings Rob and I both felt! Old friends smiled, hugged, and greeted Chris and us with genuine happiness. Undoubtedly, some thought that our troubles were now behind us, forgetting in that moment of joy and love that we still live in a fallen world. Our faith in God's promise of an eternal life in heaven with Him does not remove our earthly trials. But He promises to go with us through our trials and provide us with His wisdom, comfort, and strength. I know this to be true. Otherwise, I would not have been able to sit through that church service and watch Chris walk down the aisle. That's how tense I felt. Not only was I afraid Chris might explode, but I was afraid I would explode. I don't think the three of us breathed until we finally escorted Chris out of the church building and were sitting in the car.

Soon after his baptism Chris began to loudly proclaim that he was God. He would yell, "I am God!" over and over to everyone in the family. Nine days after his baptism, he sent a note to his psychiatrist stating, "I am on the verge of mathematically proving the existence of God." In an extremely fanatical tone of voice, he quoted scriptures out of context that sounded judgmental and damning. His movements were scary. He was jumping and posturing, theatrical and dramatic. Rob and I truly did not know what to think or what to do. We fell back on our PDAP training. We told Chris to go upstairs and calm down or we would leave the room. We were not going to stay in his presence when he was out of control. This at least provided all of us with a level of safety when we did not know whether this moment was going to escalate into something dangerous.

Full-Blown Psychosis Arrives

For the next three months Chris's behavior became more and more bizarre. By April, Chris had decided to stop seeing his counselor and psychiatrist and had stopped taking his meds. I met with the psychiatrist alone for Chris's May 29 appointment. I was hoping to gain some insight into why Chris had stopped coming to the psychiatrist and was no longer taking any medication. Because Chris was no longer a minor, the doctor held back the details but told me that they had had a "therapeutic rupture." I took that to mean that in his manic, psychotic state, Chris had gotten angry at his doctor and simply was refusing to come. From reviewing Chris's medical records, I learned later that the doctor had discontinued the Adderall prescription in April until Chris's mood stabilized. This likely triggered Chris's refusal to stay in treatment. He'd been taking 60 mg of Adderall per day along with Risperdal (for psychosis), Depakote (for mania), and Celexa (for depression). He was disappointed that the Adderall had been discontinued because he thought it gave him back the energy taken away by the antidepressant and antipsychotic medications. He felt as if those medications prevented him from being able to write or read due to the drowsiness they caused. Medication noncompliance always had been and still was a problem for Chris and in the long run may have contributed to the severity of his mental illness. It was and is against medical advice to stop taking psychotropic medications suddenly, but Chris was determined to follow only his own advice.

Whispers Become Hallucinations and Delusions of Telepathy

The whispers Chris heard before Christmas began to manifest as auditory hallucinations and critical, derogatory voices. These were symptoms of psychosis and were present along with the mania. Fixed delusions of telepathy appeared. Chris was paranoid that the cable company had installed bugs in the cable boxes. He thought the television and radio were broadcasting his thoughts out to the world and were putting thoughts into his head. He believed that the police, actually "fake police," were going to come into our house, arrest him, and torture him. He slept with a steel rod and a baseball bat wedged between his mattress and bed rail so he could protect himself when the intruders came. I found these objects when changing his sheets and asked him about them. He told me they were for protection when the fake police came to get him. He related that to me in a perfectly calm voice as if it were totally logical.

Delusional decision-making processes also became part of Chris's thinking. The color of a car he would pass on the road dictated some decision he was contemplating. Should he meet his friends for coffee or stay home and read? He saw a yellow car, and that meant he would go for coffee. Should he buy a new pair of Converse tennis shoes or save his money? He saw a green car, which meant save the money. He would notice a car and watch it to see whether it turned right or left. The direction cars took when turning also became a decision-making point for him. Next, Chris decided that he should not make any left turns when driving. Turning right and going straight were the only ways he would go when he was driving. Eventually this kind of thinking and decision making led to Chris's refusing to drive at all. Driving became too complicated—trying to watch car colors, noticing left and right turns, and going only straight or turning right. These "rules" controlled him and ultimately contributed to his becoming almost totally withdrawn and housebound.

Letter to the IRS

After I found the rod and bat, Chris later told me more about why he was feeling so paranoid. He had written a letter to the IRS, accusing the government of various conspiracies. I never saw the letter, but he insisted that he had mailed it and that it had been very accusatory. He seemed to regret sending the letter because now the government knew his name and address. He was sure that the FBI was going to come after him. I admit that I was worried about what Chris might have written. Did he make threats that could open him up to some kind of investigation?

One evening close to Easter, Chris ran into the house yelling that he was going to Las Vegas. He had a new girlfriend, whom we had just met. She was a college student, and Chris had met her during his brief college tenure. She and another friend wanted to take a car trip to Las Vegas during spring break and invited Chris. He quickly grabbed some clothes, was out the front door, and gone. All he said to us was that he had seen a yellow car, so he knew he was supposed to go along on the trip. After three days he returned home tired and beleaguered looking. His girlfriend told us it had been a rough trip with Chris. At one point while camping outside at night, Chris was sure that the FBI was stalking him in the woods. He apparently was close to going berserk. He finally calmed down when she threatened to leave him there in the woods. They did finish the trip to Las Vegas, turned around, and came back home. Surprisingly, it did not finish the relationship between Chris and his girlfriend. That would turn out to be a blessing in the coming weeks.

11

Joy and Terror

Chris's mood was changing. After the Las Vegas trip, he became quiet and rarely went out of the house. He dropped his one college course, English, midsemester. While taking the English course, he had become a prolific journal writer and now spent many hours writing, studying tarot cards, and reading books on the occult as well as the Bible. This went on for four or five weeks, until the end of May. Rob and I had our usual end-of-school pileup of stress and deadlines. We had gained stamina handling this seasonal upturn in our jobs while still managing to monitor Chris's mental health. As he seemed to be moving into a depression and had suddenly stopped his treatment and medication, we again prayed that we could make it through our transitions without major upheaval. Rob was closing out one semester of grades for five courses and getting ready to teach two summer courses. Along with working, I began taking additional graduate courses at night during the spring to complete an additional educational administrator's certificate. I had already registered for one summer school course and had one week off between ending work for this school year and starting my new summer class.

This part of our roller-coaster ride coincided with Will's approaching marriage in mid-June. I was thankful I was the mother of the groom and not the mother of the bride. Our biggest responsibility was to plan the rehearsal dinner, smile, and go along with his bride's plans. It was a joyful time. Both families were happy about the coming event. In all honesty Rob did most of the planning for the rehearsal dinner. He made all the phone calls and arrangements. I did what he told me to do. He was a very gifted father of the groom!

Gulf Coast weather played a role in my story during the early part of June. Life goes on, as I said. As we were dealing with all of our own Malone-made stress, a tropical storm named Allison created havoc in Houston and Harris County for several days. The local CBS news station summarized the June 4, 2001, storm as follows:

- Tropical Storm Allison devastated the Houston area with forty inches of rain.
- The floodwaters shut down hospitals, destroyed thousands of homes and killed twenty-three people in Texas.
- Buses and big rigs were under water on Interstate 10 and other highways.
- The storm caused flooding the first time it passed over the Bayou City on June 4, 2001. But the worst flooding came a few days later when it turned around and targeted Houston again.
- Allison caused $5.5 billion in damages and taught Houstonians that tropical storms can be even more dangerous than hurricanes.[1]

That storm is an important event for me because it marks the beginning of Chris's devastating decline into the most severe form of mental illness. Our house did not flood, nor did our cars stall out. We periodically lost power for a few minutes, but for the most part Rob and I were at home feeling safe, content to stay inside and watch weather news on TV. Chris was not home.

As the news article above states, the storm came and then came again. Before Allison's turnaround, Chris had left the house without letting us know where he was going. I had heard the front door slam on Thursday afternoon, and I knew Chris had left, but that is all I knew. By dinnertime we had not heard from him, nor did he come home. By Friday the storm reports grew continually more ominous. Almost all the roads in the Houston area were impassable. People were stranded everywhere.

Chris did not return that night, during the day on Saturday, or Saturday night. Phone land lines were not working. Cell phones were not prevalent in 2001. We could not go out in our car to look for him at friends' houses. We waited, watched television, and prayed.

At 6:30 p.m. Sunday, Chris and his girlfriend (from the Las Vegas trip) walked in our front door. We were so relieved to see him, but we also noticed that both of his forearms were wrapped in white bandages. Our reunion suddenly turned very sobering. Rob and I knew what those bandages meant. Chris had slit both wrists on Thursday afternoon while at home and then had called his girlfriend to tell her. She'd quickly come to our house, picked him up, and taken him with her. That was the slamming door I had heard on Thursday. They did not go to an emergency room but drove to her college apartment in Huntsville, where she managed to stop the bleeding and bandage both of Chris's arms. They stayed at her apartment until Allison's onslaught began to diminish on Sunday afternoon. She was finally able to persuade Chris to come home and tell us what he had done.

> This was the first of five suicide attempts and gestures Chris would make in 2001, all because of his delusions of telepathy and government torture.

The four of us sat quietly in our living room while Chris talked about feeling scared, paranoid, and depressed. As far as I knew, he had stopped the self-abusive cutting on his body that he had done in high school. This was different. He trembled when he told us about his fear of being arrested and tortured by the government because of his letter to the IRS. This was the first of five suicide attempts and gestures Chris would make in 2001, all because of his delusions of telepathy and government torture. During this conversation we talked to Chris about going into the hospital so he could get some help for the depression. He had not been in any kind of treatment or on medication since April, and prior to this we had seen the psychotic symptoms and manic mood swing start up after Christmas, six months before. Apparently his girlfriend had also talked to him about taking this step before they had returned to our house. She and Rob encouraged Chris to take this voluntary step to help himself while I called his psychiatrist to ask for a hospital referral, which was a major problem because of Tropical Storm Allison.

Houston's entire Texas Medical Center was closed due to flooding. Consequently, outlying hospitals were taking all patients, both new and those transferred from the medical center. There basically was very little room in the inn. Finally after several phone calls, I located an available bed at a psychiatric hospital in far southwest Houston. Rob and I took Chris there late Sunday night. He was admitted and placed on suicide watch. We went home exhausted but relieved that he was in a safe place.

With Will's wedding just six days away, we expected him home soon. Chris was going to be one of Will's groomsmen. He had already been fitted for his tuxedo. Rob and I reminded ourselves to ask the doctor if Chris would be able to participate in the wedding. We wanted Will's wedding to be the dream it was planned to be, and that meant all our family would be present and happy. With Chris in the hospital and safe, Rob and I could handle our last-minute wedding duties, relax, and look forward to this most special weekend. I had a few morning classes and Rob had a few evening classes, but our afternoons were ours together to get ready for Saturday.

Our sense of relief lasted two days. As a group counseling session was ending on the morning of Chris's third day at the hospital, he heard a voice in his head telling him, "Kill yourself on TV." Chris interpreted the voice literally. He ran and jumped on top of a large television set sitting on a table and dived headfirst onto the tile floor. The group counselor and other staff were present when Chris did this. No one tried to stop him. He had moved too fast. They quickly ran to him as he lay on the floor stunned and bleeding from his head. Nursing staff and administrators were summoned, 911 was called, and Chris was taken to a nearby medical hospital emergency room by ambulance.

The hospital was in a somewhat chaotic state, again because of overcrowding due to Allison and the presence of many doctors and nurses who were unfamiliar with procedures, names, and faces at that hospital. Many hospital staff and medical personnel were present who usually worked downtown at the medical center. As a result we were not notified of Chris's injury until that evening. Rob and I drove to the hospital and found Chris in the emergency room. He had a large gash, closed with staples, and a bump on the very top of his head. Chris was weak and confused but was released and transported by ambulance to the psychiatric hospital. Since it was late, we did not follow him but instead drove home in a state of semishock. How could this have happened while Chris was supposedly on suicide watch in a psychiatric hospital?

The following day Rob and I went about our routine, placing one foot in front of the other as we had learned to do, no matter the crisis. I went to my class. Rob was at home preparing for his evening class. While in class I got a message to call home. I left my classroom to find a phone and called Rob. His news was totally shocking. He had received a phone call from the hospital telling him that the emergency room had called back this morning and instructed them to bring Chris immediately back to the hospital by ambulance. On more thorough examination of his X-rays, it had been determined that Chris had broken his neck when he dived from the TV set onto the tile floor the day before. Rob was calm when he delivered this message to me. He had had time to get control of himself before he called me and told me everything the doctor had said. He had spoken with the neurosurgeon that would be doing the surgery. This doctor was a highly regarded specialist in the medical center and was at the suburban hospital because of the extensive storm damage downtown. As soon as an operating room became available, Chris would have a halo surgically implanted to stabilize his head and neck. He had broken the fifth cervical vertebra. The doctor had reassured Rob that there did not appear to be any damage to the spinal cord and that Chris would recover completely. Our blessing from God was that He had protected Chris from further injury during his night of sleep after returning to the psychiatric hospital. I walked back into my classroom to pick up my purse and books. My friend asked if everything was all right, and I simply mumbled, "Chris broke his neck" and walked out.

It was now Thursday, two days before Will's wedding. For sure Chris would not be a groomsman now and would not walk me, as the mother of the groom, down the aisle. Rob called and canceled Chris's tuxedo. Will contacted another college friend who gladly accepted the late invitation to serve in the wedding. I still had not hemmed my dress. We had not given the rehearsal dinner a thought that entire week. Rob called the event coordinator to bring her up to date on our circumstances. She was so kind and compassionate! She did not want us to worry about a thing for our Friday evening rehearsal dinner and party. Will's fiancée and her family were totally understanding of our situation too and let us know they would take care of anything that came up, whether on our watch or theirs.

> The first staff member who had gone to Chris's aid said he told her, "A voice told me to kill myself on TV."

Midday on Thursday, Rob and I went to the hospital to have a case conference with the staff on duty at the time of Chris's injury. I admit that we were still in such a state of shock and under so much stress that we only wanted details of how this had happened, what Chris had said, and how he was acting now that he had returned with the halo. They had increased the suicidal watch of Chris to the highest level. When we visited with Chris, the psychiatric tech sat with us in the room. He never left Chris's side during his shift, and a tech was assigned to be with Chris twenty-four hours a day. The therapist who had been conducting the group session almost seemed as subdued about Chris as I felt. She was stunned by what Chris had done and was very concerned about his well-being. The first staff member who had gone to Chris's aid said he told her, "A voice told me to kill myself on TV." I wanted to cry when she told us this.

One of the hospital's biggest worries was that Chris was potentially in danger because of the halo. They had moved him into a psychiatric intensive care unit from the regular unit where he had first been admitted on Sunday night. Technically, this was the level of care he needed, but the other patients in this unit were also severely ill with psychotic disorders. They might see Chris as a threat precisely because of the unusual contraption on his head and neck. Rob and I agreed that Chris was better off in the regular unit and that the hospital would continue the high level of suicide watch.

The following day was Friday, the day of the rehearsal dinner. Rob taught on Friday morning, but I did not have a class, so I stayed home and packed for the weekend. We decided to make a quick visit to see Chris at the hospital before leaving for the wedding rehearsal and dinner. Friday is always the worst traffic day in Houston, something that was far from our consciousness that day. Our house was located between the hospital in far southwest Houston and Lake Conroe, forty miles north of us, where the wedding was to be held. That made the hospital and Chris about a hundred miles from the wedding site. We arrived at the wedding rehearsal site just as everyone was leaving to go to the hotel for our dinner! We put a smile on our faces, hugged everyone, and turned our car around to head for the hotel and the dinner we were hosting. I had no idea what to expect since neither of us had talked to the event coordinator after alerting her on Thursday morning about the chaos in our life.

Not to worry is what she'd said, and she meant it! The room was beautiful. The views out the windows were perfect. The tables for our forty guests glittered with mirrors, crystal, pearls, and candles. The meal was delicious. The wine we bought flowed, and the father of the bride contributed a keg of beer. Rob managed to dig deep down to the joy and love he felt for Will and gave a thoroughly funny, more-than-satisfactory impromptu toast for our son. The young people partied much later than Rob and I did, but everyone was staying in the hotel for the night. I felt that all were safe, and I collapsed into my bed, leaving my dress still to be hemmed on Saturday, the day of the wedding.

Rob and I made it to the wedding on time. I had hemmed my dress, but it came loose during the reception. I didn't care. I smiled until my jaws ached. Will's friend who took Chris's place in escorting me was kind and caring. To this day he has a special place in my heart for the role he played in my life during Chris's sad absence.

12

Suicidal Thoughts Reign

Chris remained in the hospital for twenty days and continued in an outpatient hospital program for two additional weeks following his Tropical Storm Allison admission. This most recent attempt at suicide, responding to the command in his head to kill himself on TV, shook us more than any other episode we had experienced on the roller coaster of Chris's mental illness. This was the event that brought me to recognize the reality that I could not "fix" Chris. If he were healed from this illness, it would not be a result of anything Rob or I did. We prayed and listened for God's wisdom. We had always fought, persevered, and stood up to the challenge. That was what God still seemed to be telling us to do, but we also had to understand that healing, saving, and fixing were not in our power and never had been. We needed to give this over to Him, to put ourselves and Chris in God's arms. We also came to the point of accepting that neither medicine nor psychology had a good handle on this disease. Mental illness could be fatal to Chris at any moment and without warning, even though he was receiving the best possible treatment available. Not the best treatment, but the best possible treatment available to us in Houston, Texas, in 2001.

A New Diagnosis

Everyone was shaken by what Chris had done in breaking his neck. Seeing him in the halo was a sobering reminder of the serious harm mental illness can cause in an instant. The fact that Chris caused his broken neck because of auditory hallucinations revealed a far greater risk to him from his illness than did the slashing of his wrists when he was first admitted. Intuitively, Rob and I knew this. We had seen too much on this ride not to recognize a dangerous escalation in Chris's mental illness. Chris had a wonderful psychiatrist while in the hospital. He explained to us with great patience and compassion that the command Chris heard in his head to "kill yourself" was the doctor's greatest concern. The voices in his head were a significant factor that prompted the psychiatrist to record a new diagnosis for Chris's illness—schizoaffective disorder, bipolar type.

> The words would come apart in his head with the letters becoming all mixed up and out of order. It felt to him as if his ability to think was being broken down by the voices.

Rob and I had informed ourselves as much as possible by reading about mental illness and talking to professionals in the field. But *schizoaffective* was a totally new term to us. The doctor explained that the illness was severe with psychotic features and had symptoms typical of mood disorders (like bipolar disorder) and thought disorders (like schizophrenia). *Psychotic features* referred to the active hallucinations and prevalence of paranoid delusions in Chris's mind that were preventing him from functioning normally in life and were literally causing him psychic pain and mental confusion. We were very familiar with the mood swings, both mania and depression. As we applied this new information about thought disorders and psychotic features, we saw how these had been present in Chris for at least the past six months. The delusions of telepathy, paranoia of fake police, whispers in his head, claims of being God, and weird decision-making rules about car colors and left/right turns were all clear symptoms of a chronic and serious thought disorder. He told me that the voices changed up words in his head. *Know* would become *k now.* The words would come apart in his head with the letters becoming all mixed up and out of order. It felt to him as if his ability to think was being broken down by the voices.

Shortly before this hospital stay, I had noticed that Chris would manipulate letters in words that gave the word a new meaning. He turned *Malone* into *Mal* (bad) *One.* He was Bad One. Then *M* (Im) turned into *I'm alone.* Chris felt alone and scared. This kind of writing, which I had seen in his journal, now made bizarre sense to me. I did not understand the mystery of Chris's mental illness, but sometimes he was able to give me a small piece of the puzzle.

The Halo

Wearing the halo was extremely tiring for Chris. He rested much of the time in his room. The halo was attached to his skull by four screws, two over his eyebrows and two behind his ears. At shoulder level the halo bars were attached to a semihard, fleece-lined, full-torso vest, which Chris could not take off. The vest was heavy and hot and offered little flexibility; Chris couldn't turn his head or move his neck in any direction. He rested and slept sitting up in a chair, propped up with pillows. The screw holes had to be cleaned several times a day to prevent infection. All bathing was with a washcloth and warm, soapy water—no tub baths or showers. Chris could not take care of his personal hygiene by himself and had to have help.

He wore the halo for four months and had periodic CT scans to check for healing. I met the neurosurgeon one time, when the halo surgery was first performed. Rob took Chris to all his doctor checkups and halo-adjusting orthotic appointments except the last one. I took Chris to the last orthotic appointment, when the halo was removed, and the neurosurgeon finally discharged him.

Our summer was rather subdued, a time of just putting one foot in front of the other. I finished my course work, and Rob taught summer school both sessions. With Chris's halo off, we took a short trip to Dallas and spent a day at the Texas State Fair. Chris remained under the care of the psychiatrist from the hospital. After his discharge from the day hospital program, Chris started seeing his therapist again for regular therapy. The thing I feared, but knew was probably true, was that the voices were a constant in Chris's head. He was quiet and seemed to be far away in his thoughts. Was he hearing more commands to hurt himself? Rob and I conscientiously watched over Chris, often referred to by professionals as "hypervigilant"—too vigilant, too tightly wound with concern while we waited for the next dangerous episode for Chris.

This was a period of ambivalence for me. I felt a peace about recognizing that I was not in charge in this matter and that Chris was in God's hands. This acceptance also left me knowing there was a high likelihood that we would lose Chris, perhaps sooner rather than later. During that time period Rob and I both were prescribed antidepressant medications as well. We had to be able to sleep and go about our daily business. If we crashed, where would that leave Chris? My doctor told me not to worry about my recent weight gain; he said I had enough to deal with already. That was a shocker coming from an MD!

Unexpectedly, the psychiatrist we'd liked so much from the hospital dropped off our insurance provider panel on September 1. This was a huge disappointment. We could not afford to continue with him treating Chris on a private pay basis, so Chris, Rob, and I decided together to contact the psychiatrist Chris had been with earlier in the year before his hospital admission, despite the therapeutic rupture in April. We reconnected with this psychiatrist, and Chris began his appointments in September while continuing to see his therapist for counseling.

On September 11, 2001, America was attacked by al-Qaeda terrorists. Rob and I had left the house at our regular times that morning while Chris in his halo was still in bed asleep. I heard the news of the first plane crash on the radio as I was driving to work. The second plane crashed into the second tower just after I arrived at my office. We were all shocked, horrified, and confused. The news continued to unfold the horrific story of the act of war that was aimed at killing thousands of American citizens. My morning in the school district ran rampant with all sorts of e-mails, phone calls, notes, and ad hoc meetings about preparation and protection of children and reassurance to parents. Crisis plans were implemented, and many important decisions and plans had to be made, especially with the initial news that the Houston oil and chemical industries were also possible targets of terrorists. As soon as I could take a break, I got in my car and quickly drove home. I was afraid that if Chris saw this news on television, he would somehow connect these events to his telepathy delusions and paranoia about the government. When I arrived home, Rob was also just pulling into the driveway. Both of us had had the same fear for Chris but were unable to get in touch with each other. Rob's classes had been dismissed early, and he had immediately returned home. We both went upstairs to check on Chris and found him still asleep. What a relief! We woke him up and told him what had happened. Then we heated up a can of soup and sat down to have a quick lunch together, enjoying a precious moment of normalcy in a crazy world. Rob stayed home with Chris, and I returned to work. One step at a time, life goes on.

One step at a time, life goes on.

In the following three months as we approached Thanksgiving and then Christmas, Chris remained depressed and attempted suicide three more times, two minor gestures and one major episode. They all involved Chris cutting his wrists with a knife during the night. With the first event, I found Chris sitting on the floor in his room, holding a knife and staring at his bleeding wrists. I took him to our family doctor for bandaging, and he recommended that Chris see his psychiatrist. When I got home, I called the psychiatrist and received directions to tweak Chris's medication and then bring him in on the date of his next appointment. The second gesture happened on the Friday following Thanksgiving. Again I took Chris to the family doctor but saw someone new because of the holiday. I felt a little scolded by the new doctor for not jumping at his suggestion to go to the emergency room for a psychiatric examination. I declined, opting for butterfly stitches and my promise to call Chris's psychiatrist. We had already planned to have our Thanksgiving celebration on Friday because Rob's sister and father were coming in from out of town to join us for the holiday. When Chris and I returned home, I went to the kitchen and Chris went to his room. Rob had gotten in touch with his dad and had requested that we set dinner back two hours. Our guests agreed, and we went on with the plans. We said nothing about our errand to the doctor's office earlier that day. Chris wore long sleeves, and no bandages showed. We even took the customary family holiday pictures. Life goes on.

Chris's depression continued to become more and more severe. About two weeks later, on December 13, he cut his wrists again. It was around 9:00 p.m. Rob and I were downstairs watching TV when we heard a loud clunk upstairs. I went up to check on Chris and found him standing in his underwear at the top of the stairs. He was holding a large bloody knife, with blood dripping heavily from both hands. I reached for Chris's arm and saw a deep cut. I screamed to Rob for help, told Chris to sit down, and grabbed two clean pillowcases from a linen closet. I quickly bound Chris's wrists with the pillowcases and took the knife away from him. Chris looked as if he were in a trance. He had a very small smile on his face and just sat there while I bandaged him and Rob dressed him. Rob sat on the stairs hugging Chris close to him while I called 911. Rob then went outside to wait for the ambulance, and I took his place holding Chris. I asked why he had hurt himself. He said in a weak, tentative voice that he was afraid that terrorists were going to torture him and cut him in two with a chain saw. He did not want to live through the torture. Holding Chris in my arms and hearing his fears took me back to comforting my children from hurts and scary things when they were very young. But I didn't feel confident this time as I had some twenty years before as a young mother. I was scared too. His bleeding arms made this demon psychosis feel all too real.

I was right about the severity of the cuts. The ER doctor showed us bare wrist bone when he examined Chris. The wrists kept bleeding profusely. The doctor put in temporary staples and sent a referral to an orthopedic surgeon, a hand specialist. In the meantime I called Chris's psychiatrist and told him what had happened. He contacted the psychiatric hospital to have Chris admitted after he was medically stabilized at the ER.

After Chris was stapled, we had a long wait for the ambulance that was to take him basically across the street to the psychiatric hospital. Because of his mental instability, that was the only way he could be transported. Chris became agitated with the wait, so agitated that he tried to run out of the ER room toward the street. Rob wrestled with him and tried to restrain him without injuring his wrists further. I yelled for security, and a police officer ran up and helped Rob return Chris to a treatment room, where the officer stayed. He was a kind, young officer and spoke in a reassuring way to Chris. His presence allowed Rob and me to catch our breath for a few moments. I worried that Chris's delusions would cause him to see this police officer as a torturer. The psychiatrist ordered a sedative for Chris, and he calmed down. Near 4:30 a.m. the ambulance finally arrived to take Chris for admission to the next hospital across the street. Chris became wary again and did not want to get into the ambulance. The paramedic agreed to let Rob ride with Chris to reassure him, and I drove our car.

The following morning, December 14, was a workday for me and was the day of my department's Christmas luncheon at a local restaurant. Rob and I did not get home from the hospital until 6:00 a.m., and since I had received no sleep, I called in and left a message that I would come in to work in time for the luncheon. At 10:00 a.m. my secretary called me at home to remind me that I had the check to pay the restaurant. I had been awake about thirty minutes following my three hours of sleep and was still drinking morning coffee. I quickly threw on clothes and drove to the office. My secretary was standing outside waiting for me. I parked in a space reserved for the handicapped and drove right into the sign marking the space. I had not told my secretary what had happened to Chris, only that we had taken him to the ER and did not get home until 6:00 a.m. She saw me hit and bend the sign pole and was astonished. She said, “Benny, what did you just do?!” I calmly said, “I hit the pole.” Then I handed her the check and got back in my car. I needed to return home, shower, and get dressed for work. I'm pretty sure that I was in a kind of shock that morning. I felt as if I were moving by remote control. Some part of my brain was getting me where I needed to be, but my emotions were numb.

I was in a kind of shock that morning. I felt as if I were moving by remote control. Some part of my brain was getting me where I needed to be, but my emotions were numb.

Later that day Rob and I met with the hand surgeon and got the word on the damage to Chris's wrists. He had severed nerves and tendons in both wrists. Surgery was required, and the doctor had already scheduled it. Plans were made to transfer Chris from the psychiatric facility back to the first hospital.

Connecting with the County and State Mental Health Systems

The attending psychiatrist went to court to get a judge's order to keep Chris hospitalized. It is hard to believe, but this was considered a voluntary placement by Chris himself. If he decided to walk out of the psychiatric hospital, no one could stop him. Chris's regular therapist was also on staff at the psychiatric hospital and personally knew of his long history of mental illness and his previous episodes of seriously endangering himself. With the doctor's recommendation and the therapist's perseverance and determination, a long-term hospital placement at Rusk State Hospital was arranged. There was only one state hospital bed available for a Harris County resident, and Chris got it! We had one more ambulance ride in front of us. Chris was discharged by the hand surgeon on December 22 and later that day was transported to the state hospital in Rusk, Texas. This was a court-ordered placement.

Again we had to wait for an ambulance, which finally arrived around midnight. We followed the ambulance in our car while it transported Chris to Rusk. It was shortly after 3:00 a.m. when we all arrived. We took just a few minutes to meet the admissions on-call social worker and told Chris that we would return two days later with some version of Christmas dinner, provided he was allowed to have a visit. The social worker agreed to let us know as soon as possible about the visit since it would have to be approved by the attending psychiatrist. We said weary good-byes and got in our car to make the three-hour return trip home.

The psychiatrist did approve our Christmas Day visit. We bought fried chicken and french fries along the road at a fast food restaurant, and I brought some of the fudge that I had made in between our ambulance and surgery days. I always made candy for my office friends at Christmas and had managed to keep this tradition.

Chris remained at Rusk for almost three months. We visited a few times but decided that these visits needed to be limited for everyone's benefit. Rob and I had met with Chris's therapist several times prior to his transfer to Rusk, and she strongly encouraged us to set boundaries that allowed us to provide some self-care. At this point in our lives, Rob and I began to feel that Chris had taken about all we had to give. We knew he was in the safest possible place for the time being. We also knew that God, not us, was in charge, and that was a huge blessing of self-care on its own.

I would love to say that Chris got well while at the hospital, but he didn't. He did get better, which was very encouraging. Chris earned the privilege of having a job, for which he was paid minimum wage. He took life skills classes and had therapy sessions to attend on a daily basis. He worked at his job about four hours a week. The staff liked Chris. His quiet, friendly manner and sense of responsibility were the best indicators that the treatment was being successful. We saw this in him on our visits, and it was good.

We no longer got excited at signs of recovery, but our hope and emotional energy gradually strengthened. However, improvement was also the first indicator for discharge from the hospital. I don't know how long it would have taken for Chris to return to an actual state of complete wellness—that is, stability of his mood and thought disorders and ultimately the ability to function independently in the world—but the one and only state hospital bed for a Harris County resident was undoubtedly needed by someone else in a severely psychotic state. Chris was discharged on March 15, 2002, with a referral to Harris County Mental Health Mental Retardation Authority (MHMRA) for follow-up outpatient care.

It didn't take long for old patterns to return. Chris was not reliable in taking his medication. So in November 2002, eight months after his discharge from Rusk, Chris swung to the manic side and decided he no longer needed treatment from MHMRA. By April 2003, he was psychotic again and very depressed. He talked repeatedly of killing himself. We convinced him to go in the hospital to get stabilized on medication again. We had a harried ride to Houston's medical center downtown to seek emergency psychiatric care for Chris at the Harris County NeuroPsychiatric Center (NPC). Along the way he tried to open the car door and jump out. I stopped the car, and somehow Rob and I prevented him from getting hurt. For the rest of the forty-five-minute ride, Chris sat on his knees, facing backward in the front passenger seat while tightly gripping the headrest, and stared at Rob. Rob kept talking calmly and reassuringly to Chris from the backseat while I drove. Rob was blessed with a great voice. It sounded calm, deep, and powerful. I called it his radio voice. He uttered his words to Chris with the love and intense compassion we both felt for our deeply troubled son. As Rob spoke from his heart in his deep voice, I started to feel calmer too. The sound of his voice helped me to focus on getting us safely through Houston traffic as quickly as possible. That afternoon Rob's voice was an unexpected tool in our skills toolbox for managing Chris's mental illness—another blessing from God, freely given.

When we arrived at NPC, Chris refused to go inside because he saw a police officer on the grounds near the building's entrance. We sat on a bench in a courtyard and tried to convince Chris that he was safe. I went inside to try to have him admitted but was told he had to walk in on his own *or* be delivered by court order *or* be brought in by a police officer if Chris demonstrated harm to himself or others in the courtyard. What a brick wall! God gave me the peace not to scream. And He gave me the perseverance to remain with the nurse persuading, explaining, practically begging until she got permission from a doctor to walk out the door to meet Chris in the courtyard. Chris calmly let her take his temperature and blood pressure and put a wristband on his arm. We then all walked into the hospital.

What a brick wall! God gave me the peace not to scream. And He gave me the perseverance to remain with the nurse, persuading, explaining, practically begging until she got permission from a doctor to walk out the door to meet Chris in the courtyard.

Chris was admitted for observation. The attending psychiatrist recommended hospitalization after interviewing the three of us and examining Chris. Rob and I agreed. She filed the paperwork for a court order for involuntary placement. Rob and I drove home exhausted while another mental health professional took over care of our son and had him transported to Harris County Psychiatric Center (HCPC). That was his first stay in this particular psychiatric hospital. Over a nine-year period, Chris was hospitalized ten times in five different psychiatric hospitals. HCPC was number five. Unknown to us, hospitals six and seven were still in his future.

Chris was discharged from HCPC ten days later on medication but still very psychotic. He was referred again for outpatient treatment at MHMRA. Rob made the intake appointment for a Friday two weeks away. On the morning of the appointment, I went upstairs to check on Chris as I did every morning before I got ready for work. I found him on the floor unconscious, stiff, and immovable. I could not wake him up. I could not straighten out his arms, legs, or torso. My first thought was that he was dead. I screamed to Rob, who ran upstairs. He could not move Chris either. I called 911, and an ambulance arrived quickly, shortly after 7:30 a.m. Chris was breathing, and the paramedics placed him, still unconscious, in his stiffened posture on the stretcher. Lights and sirens came on outside our house again as Chris was rushed to the hospital. A lot happened in the next four days as Chris remained in a coma in ICU. We learned that he had overdosed on the antipsychotic medication Zyprexa.

I do not know why Chris did not die as a result of this overdose. Later he told us he thought that MHMRA was an instrument of the government determined to take over his mind through telepathy. He was totally paranoid and afraid and did not want to go to his appointment. Chris's bizarre thoughts and psychotic symptoms almost killed him.

13

Calm Before the Psychotic Storm

After the Zyprexa overdose and coma and because of Chris's paranoia regarding MHMRA as a government entity, Rob and I decided to contact the psychiatrist who was treating Chris before his Rusk hospitalization. We had first started with this doctor when Chris was in high school and had returned to him a few months after losing the Tropical Storm Allison psychiatrist from our insurance panel. He had been Chris's psychiatrist off and on for the past five years. While Chris had worked with different psychiatrists, largely due to ten hospitalizations, we had stayed with the same licensed professional counselor who had been Chris's therapist since his first hospitalization at age fifteen. While Chris was her designated client, she also was a wonderful adviser and sounding board for us. When we first started seeing her with Chris, our sessions involved parenting, limit setting, and communication strategies for us as parents of a teenager. She played a mediator's role when we had a family counseling session with all of us present.

Later, as Chris's illness became more severe and more dangerous, she became a mental health and illness educator as well as an empathetic, wise listening ear. Chris's therapist respected his confidentiality as he got older, and he trusted her. I'm sure she knew things about Chris that we did not know or that we learned after she did. Our continued involvement with her supported us in keeping the best communication lines possible with Chris. I saw her be calm, objective, caring, and firm. She seemed to know what our family needed and was the ultimate mental health professional. We were always at ease with her, friendly but never friends in the usual sense. She encouraged us and guided us to do our job. That was one of the healthiest relationships I have had in my life.

Keeping Chris in therapy also demanded an outstanding relationship with our insurance provider. We were able to designate his sessions as hospital outpatient therapy, which had more lenient limitations than routine counseling sessions or hospitalizations did. Chris saw the therapist every two to three weeks at her hospital office for two years, until the month of Rob's death. While she was confidential about Chris's conversations with her, she willingly listened to our description of family events and difficulties at home. She could talk to Chris about these issues and guide him in better ways to cope with his stress. She would always follow up on what was discussed at a previous session, giving Chris a continuous thread of healthy support to hang on to between sessions.

This two-year period in Chris's life, June 2003 to June 2005, was a time of extreme withdrawal for him. He stopped driving, stopped meeting with friends, and rarely came out of his upstairs bedroom. His primary outside activity was his monthly visit to the psychiatrist and his counseling sessions. At home he wrote in journals prolifically. He would leave them out, and I would look at them when I went into his room. This was not a secret from Chris. I think he wanted me to read his journals. He almost stopped communicating verbally with us about anything other than asking, "What's for dinner?" Glancing through his journals gave me the only insight I had into his thinking. He wrote from page edge to page edge, top to bottom, side to side, and front to back in tiny print with crisp black ink. I still have a large plastic container full of his journals. They clearly depict his mental confusion as well as his bouts of mania and depression.

With the therapist's encouragement, I began the application process for Social Security Disability benefits on Chris's behalf.

With the therapist's encouragement, I began the application process for Social Security Disability benefits on Chris's behalf. I knew nothing about that possible resource except what I had read in the newspaper. The *Houston Chronicle* had reported that applications for disability benefits were routinely denied for three years or longer if and when any approvals were granted in Harris County. This bureaucratic process required multiple appeals from families and individuals seeking approval of benefits. I did not expect this to be even a possibility for Chris; plus I did not think I had the energy to take on this battle. So far he was still within the age range to be covered by my medical insurance. His therapist was good at looking ahead for us and seeing the whole forest. I just saw the tree that was smack-dab in my face. She reminded me of how much Rob and I and our family members on both sides had paid over the years in income tax, property tax, sales tax, and every other kind of tax levied by federal, state, and local governmental entities without ever claiming any assistance or help. We now needed help or would soon at Chris's twenty-fifth birthday. I took the therapist's advice and submitted an application. It was complicated and time intensive, not counting the many persuasive conversations I had with Chris that we were not turning "all of his information" over to the government. I admit we had to work around his fixed delusion and paranoia about the government coming after him with its terrorists.

Chris refused to sign the first application. My persuasiveness, which had worked with the nurse at NPC who eventually walked outside the doors of the psychiatric facility to admit Chris, did not work with the Social Security Administration (SSA). Thankfully, Chris's therapist persistently encouraged me to be persistent with Chris and the SSA. I suspect that she discussed this issue with Chris in their counseling sessions. He eventually signed and authorized me to complete the application process. And he was approved on the first round! From beginning to end, it took nine months for the application to be processed and approved. I had to obtain all his medical records, counseling records, and special education records. Chris's financial information, such as savings accounts and checking accounts and assets as well as current and past income history, had to be submitted. I was interviewed first, and then Chris had to come in for a personal interview with an SSA representative. Getting him out of the house for this interview was also a challenge, but Chris finally cooperated.

The final step was Chris's evaluation by an independent psychologist. We worried about that step the most. What if Chris appeared too stable to look unable to hold a job or fend for himself in the world? I should have known that God's plan had been in place all along and that there was no other possible result than approval. And why did I doubt, remembering the almost-amputated arms, the broken neck that did not paralyze, the slit wrists with tendon and nerve damage that healed, the four days of coma in the ICU with no resulting lung or brain damage? Our son was so mentally ill, how could anyone who looked at the record doubt this fact? If Chris looked stable in that SSA psychological evaluation, I bet the psychologist thought, *Good for you, Chris. You are thinking more clearly today.*

When Chris was approved, he was issued a check retroactively covering all the previous months' benefits from the original date of the disability application. Chris himself had built up a small Social Security account from his employment during and after high school. He was actually approved on his own work record. I am proud of that for Chris. Being approved for Social Security Disability benefits made him eligible for Medicare, and since he had no resources and no job at age twenty-three, he also qualified for Supplemental Security Income (SSI). A portion of our assets were attributed to him as assets, such as free room and board under our roof and our contribution to his medical care. Counting these assets, Chris met the financial cutoff for SSI by less than fifteen dollars, just barely making him eligible for Medicaid, a medical benefit for disabled indigents that covers what Medicare does not pay. I didn't care if he qualified for only fifty cents a month as a result of the Social Security Disability eligibility. He had medical coverage! A huge burden fell off our shoulders. Rob and I had faith that we could feed, shelter, and clothe the three of us as long as was necessary. Chris's medical care would have been totally out of our reach in just a few months. Ironically, his initial disability check arrived in May 2005, barely two months before Rob was killed.

Chris stayed in this kind of limbo state after the Zyprexa overdose for about fifteen months, not better but having few outbursts or attempts at self-harm. Rob and I continued to take one day at a time while we waited. Periods of stability like this had occurred before with Chris—following ninth grade and following eleventh grade. Perhaps these were patterns, but I did not discern them while we were living them. I attributed that period of relative calm to consistency in his counseling sessions and medication, the reduced hypervigilance that Rob and I had usually given, and God's blessings.

In September 2004 our roller coaster began to jump the tracks.

14

Off the Tracks in a Psychotic Storm

Chris and I had started attending support groups sponsored by the National Alliance on Mental Illness (NAMI) the summer following his Zyprexa overdose and psychiatric hospitalization. Rob could rarely attend because he taught evening classes on meeting nights. Chris attended a group for consumers of mental health services, and I attended the family support group. This participation provided a great benefit to both Chris and me. The sessions met twice a month. Chris was stable for the most part and formed relationships with other stable young adults dealing with the same debilitating mental health issues. The consumer group functioned solely as a support group. My group met for two purposes: one session was educational, followed by an informal social get-together with others in the group, and the second session was a support group. The first group meeting of the month included educational classes and presentations from lawyers and judges on topics such as guardianship, mental health patients' rights, and family law. We also heard speakers who were mental health professionals, community resource providers, and financial planning advisers who addressed the long-term support issues faced by families of a loved one with mental illness. The second session of the month was strictly for group support. We all learned many things from each other, encouraged each other, and cried with each other. This whole experience was a blessing.

By the time we had attended NAMI for a little more than a year, Chris began to change again. He stopped going with me to meetings before the end of 2004. During the period of time we had been going to NAMI, Chris's medication regimen had been changed dramatically following his Zyprexa overdose in 2003. All those changes were made by his psychiatrist while we were participating in NAMI. When Chris was discharged from the hospital in 2003, he was taking Eskalith CR (controlled release lithium carbonate) and Zyprexa, which were prescribed by the hospital psychiatrist. Lithium is a relatively simple drug that has been used for a long time to stabilize mood swings typical of bipolar disorder. Zyprexa was a newer drug used to treat psychosis, the hallmark symptom of untreated schizophrenia. Having just these two medications was a simple regimen and easy for us to dispense and monitor. The issue of Chris's noncompliance with medication was becoming more and more critical as the illness endured over time. Each time he had a major psychotic episode, with rapid mood swings, hallucinations, and delusions raging out of control, it took him longer to recover. We were well aware of the risks of off-and-on, as-you-like-it medication dosing. When Chris was first diagnosed with schizoaffective disorder after breaking his neck, the psychiatrist had told us it took at least a year to recover from psychosis and complete recovery might never occur, especially if Chris did not consistently take his medication as prescribed.

The psychiatrist had told us it took at least a year to recover from psychosis and complete recovery might never occur.

Stimulant Medications and Psychosis

During 2004 while we were in NAMI, Chris's psychiatrist changed his medication to include Abilify, Geodon, clonazepam, and Lexapro plus the Eskalith and Zyprexa originally prescribed by the hospital psychiatrist in 2003. The medications were classified as three different atypical antipsychotics, a mood stabilizer, an antianxiety medication, and a selective serotonin-reuptake inhibitor (SSRI) antidepressant. In midsummer the doctor discontinued Zyprexa and added Provigil, an atypical stimulant medication, which promotes wakefulness. Soon after Provigil was included in his daily regimen, Chris started to request that the psychiatrist prescribe Adderall instead. That worried Rob and me because of Chris's history of stimulant abuse, specifically ephedrine and amphetamines. This psychiatrist was the only psychiatrist Chris had ever seen who said that Chris also had an unusual case of attention deficit disorder (ADD), which contributed to his being unable to switch focus when concentrating. Rob and I had seen something like this type of behavior when Chris was stuck on writing the Hitler paper in college. It wasn't that he had trouble concentrating; rather he could not wind down his focus to bring the paper to an end. But since early in childhood Chris had always been determined to finish a project to perfection. I always attributed this trait to perfectionism, which was common to all four of us. Was ADD an accurate comorbid diagnosis along with the schizoaffective disorder? Was the trait attributable to some form of obsessive-compulsive disorder? Was it a personality trait that ran in our family? Or might it even be a religion-based drive that caused Chris to feel that he had to be perfect to please God?

Chris told us and the doctor that he needed the stimulant medication because of poor concentration and problems with reading and writing. He was also experiencing suicidal thoughts, auditory hallucinations, paranoia, and religious and conspiracy delusions. Chris did not like the Provigil and continued to ask for Adderall. The psychiatrist acquiesced to Chris's request, stopped the Provigil, and prescribed Adderall in mid-October 2004. The Adderall dosage was gradually increased to the point that Chris was taking both the extended-release form and the generic immediate-release D-amphetamine salt. Between the two drugs Chris's daily dosage at one point was 80 mg—40 mg of the extended release and 40 mg of the immediate release. In two more months the antipsychotic medication, Abilify, was reintroduced in order to counter Chris's severe anxiety and rapid speech pattern.

With our growing concern about Chris's decline, in October 2004 I implemented a strategy that I had learned in NAMI. I sent the doctor the first of four letters describing Chris's behavior at home and the deterioration we were seeing. While the psychiatrist did not have to report to us anything about Chris's condition because he was now an adult, there was nothing to prevent the family from documenting the behavior at home and sharing it with the mental health professional. I faxed or delivered all the letters in advance of an appointment so the psychiatrist would have our input and know our concerns. Below is part of what I wrote to the doctor in the October 6th letter.

October 6, 2004

Chris has had increasing problems with the voices. He says they come from three places. He hears a running commentary of statements like "You're caught," "Fool," "Boo hoo," and "Wake up," all in a negative tone. One time he said you were a voice in his head ridiculing him. That seemed to make him not want to tell you things . . . He has accused me of talking about him. He says he hears me laughing and making fun of him with someone else. This is not happening. He also says the children next door, the neighbor across the street, someone passing by are yelling insults at him. He gets angry at the kids and neighbors for saying these things to him . . . Chris has been more verbally abusive, especially to me. He threatens me, uses profanity, glares, yells . . . His delusions center around religious issues and telepathy . . . I'm very worried about him. He seems on the edge. He paces constantly. He is taking his meds. We are going to NAMI meetings twice a month. He sees his therapist every other week. He is not getting better. He is getting worse . . . We are not quite at our wits' end. We just expect the world to crash in on us at any time.

Big changes in Chris's aggressiveness and anger occurred in January 2005. The difference was, rather than harming himself, Chris began striking out at us. He shoved and spit at me one morning when we crossed paths in the upstairs hallway. He blocked my way and threatened to kill me. At the time he was intensely involved in reading "codes" and using a calculator to manipulate and decipher them. He thought I was invading his space as he paced in the hallway.

Big changes in Chris's aggressiveness and anger occurred in January 2005. The difference was, rather than harming himself, Chris began striking out at us.

During the next few days, Chris said often that the television was talking to him directly and that other people outside the house were talking about him. He continued to claim that the neighbor children were laughing at him and calling him names. These were the preschool-age children of our next-door neighbors, and I truly began to worry that Chris might say something that would scare them, even though he rarely left his bedroom or the house.

One morning in January, Will had called his dad on the phone just to talk. Chris interrupted Rob and asked to talk to Will for a minute. Rob heard Chris's end of the conversation and told me later that day what he had said. His comment to Will was along the lines of "If you cross me, I'll kill your firstborn. I'm serious; I will kill Seth." Seth was Will's ten-month-old son and our first grandchild. Chris had held Seth in his arms a few weeks earlier at both Thanksgiving and Christmas. Rob and Will were both shocked. Rob apologized to Will. He'd had no inkling that Chris was about to say anything like that to his brother.

The stress of keeping track of and monitoring Chris at all times was wearing for Rob and me. We decided to file for a mental health warrant, based on Chris's physically acting out, his threat to kill me, his accusations toward the neighbors' children, and his threat to Will about baby Seth. The warrant was granted the day I filed it, and two US marshals came out to the house to transport Chris to the hospital. Because of his hostility, we were afraid to try to take him to the hospital ourselves as we always had in the past. Chris did not know this was going to happen and was totally surprised when the two officers entered his bedroom. We had met them at the door, directed them to his room, and then went outside to wait. It was horrible to see the look on Chris's face when they brought him outside in handcuffs. When he was admitted to the hospital, the record described him as "very distracted, loud, sarcastic, irritable, paranoid, delusional, and experiencing auditory hallucinations." What we did was the right thing to do, but it was so hard to follow through after Rob and I had made the decision earlier in the day—not just to file for the warrant but also to have the marshals surprise Chris. Chris was no longer a skinny teenager; he was a muscular, adult male. The power behind his behavior was dangerous.

The attending psychiatrist at the hospital knew Chris from a previous admission. He immediately took Chris off all stimulant medications, recording that stimulant medications were contraindicated in a patient with psychosis. He communicated that to Chris's therapist, who continued to provide daily individual therapy for Chris while he was hospitalized. She explained this to us in a family session. She wanted to make sure that Chris's psychiatrist, to whom he would return at discharge, knew about this medication change and the reason for it. Chris was furious with everyone, but we stuck to the plan and refused to give Chris the Adderall when he returned home from the hospital.

Following that hospitalization, in mid-February I wrote my second letter to Chris's psychiatrist, not only to tell him about recent behavior at home, but also to inform him of the hospital psychiatrist's statement that Adderall was contraindicated in Chris's psychotic state. I told the doctor that we had gotten a mental health warrant and two US marshals had picked up Chris and had taken him to the hospital without our telling him in advance. Part of the letter's contents follow below.

February 16, 2005

Needless to say, Chris is pretty angry with us. He has moderated his angry outbursts somewhat (just making threats and not in our face so much), probably because we surprised him with the two marshals and the warrant . . . Since he has been home, I'm not seeing any improvement in his hearing voices and his delusions. They are bad. He thinks we are channeling, that there is another person speaking through us. Therefore, it really doesn't matter what we say. Chris puts a different interpretation on it . . . Chris has been inconsistent in taking the medication. He has threatened to stop all medication if we do not give him the Adderall. Based on his therapist's recommendation, we held off on the Adderall until the appointment with you. It has been a struggle.

When Chris went to his two-week follow-up appointment after the hospital discharge, his psychiatrist disagreed with the hospital psychiatrist's recommendation, writing in Chris's treatment notes, "Will reintroduce Adderall when anger toward family and others is reduced." I saw the doctor's decision and statement as using Adderall as a reward for Chris if he did not act out toward us. Chris was not satisfied with just this anticipation of Adderall in his future. He reacted by refusing all medication. An irrational power struggle ensued with our handing him the pills as prescribed and Chris often throwing them back at us. He had just about beaten us down at this point.

In another month I sent a third letter to the psychiatrist. The letter was dated March 21, and I faxed it just prior to one of Chris's appointments. His talk and behavior had become increasingly dangerous. The following describes what was happening at home.

March 21, 2005

For at least two weeks Chris took very little of his medication and then only sporadically. Last week he decided to take Zyprexa and Lexapro . . . He said he has a stash of Zyprexa . . . On Friday afternoon he took Zyprexa (unknown amount) and 6 mg of Xanax and had a six-pack of beer. He was staggering drunk and slept for hours. Afterward, he did not remember some of the things he said to us. He has talked about having the "right" to kill himself if he wants to, but he doesn't think he will . . . We see his mood swings very frequently, maybe every thirty minutes . . . He will seem timid and fearful and then will declare that he is our god and will tell us we are condemned.

Two weeks following this letter, another incident occurred that resulted in Chris's being hospitalized again at the psychiatric hospital. That afternoon while driving to an appointment at a school, I had a tire blow out. I called roadside assistance and had my spare tire put on, and then I called Rob, and he met me at the tire store. We waited until the new tire was mounted and then picked up Mexican food to take home for dinner. Rob and I were relieved to be home and move past my stressful afternoon. Life goes on.

As I was putting food out for us to help ourselves, Chris walked in and shoved me out of his way. I reacted with a kind of "Hey. Watch out!" attitude, and Rob also said something to Chris along the line of, "Don't treat your mother like that!" That was all it took. A fight ensued between Chris and Rob with pushing, shoving, punching, chair bumping, and door crashing. The two of them ended up on our patio, where Rob banged into our wrought-iron gate and cut his forehead. I was yelling for them to stop, but it seemed like those few moments were never going to end. I grabbed the phone and called 911. Two sheriff's deputies arrived along with an ambulance. The paramedics treated Rob's forehead cut while we talked with the deputies about whether Chris would be arrested for assault or taken for a psychiatric evaluation. We told the deputies about his mental illness, showed them all Chris's medications, described his recent hospitalization, and gave them the name of his psychiatrist. Rob, as the complainant, asked that Chris be transported to the Harris County NeuroPsychiatric Center for psychiatric evaluation rather than be arrested. The officers called in and got permission from the district attorney's office to forego arrest in favor of the emergency psychiatric evaluation. The next morning we were notified that Chris had been evaluated and was being transferred under court order to the psychiatric hospital from which he had recently been discharged. Again Rob and I felt numb, anxious, ambivalent, and exhausted. We were at a loss about what to do with Chris. Within a period of seventy-eight days, police officers had come to our home twice, handcuffed our son, and then had taken him away for court-ordered emergency psychiatric care.

With this admission to the hospital, Chris actually had two attending psychiatrists. Both noted that he was suffering from psychotic symptoms. His medications were adjusted to try to stabilize the psychosis. His usual array of hallucinations, delusions, paranoia, mania/depression, and aggression had returned. He had poor insight and judgment and was focused on getting

Adderall prescribed again. His threatening behavior during one particular counseling session was deemed too dangerous for the session to continue, and it was terminated prematurely.

During our sessions with the social worker, Rob and I began to seriously discuss long-term placement options and guardianship for Chris. We were hopeful that his recently approved disability benefits might financially help us secure an appropriate placement outside our home. The hospital psychiatrist completed the paperwork to get us started on the legal guardianship application. The guardianship application form signed by the hospital psychiatrist documented that Chris Malone was "totally incapacitated and incapable of all matters related to property and person including providing consents" for medical care, living arrangements, and financial matters. Our insurance company cooperated in granting a few extra days in the hospital so we could put the discharge plans in place for a temporary out-of-home placement.

With the social worker's help, we found a licensed personal care home. The cost was about $200 more per month than Chris's disability check. We signed forms agreeing to cover the additional charges. The home-care staff was on-site twenty-four hours a day. They administered all medication and provided a daily routine of personal hygiene monitoring, planned activities, meals and snacks, and transportation to appointments. The facility itself was neat and clean and reminded me of a boarding house. The approximately fifteen residents had separate bedrooms and common living and dining areas. We visited Chris one evening a week and went out to dinner together as a family. We were not surprised, however, that he told us he hated the place and wanted to come home. Chris stayed there for thirty days, and it was a good transition from the hospital for all of us.

The home-care staff took Chris to his first posthospitalization appointment with his psychiatrist. Rob took him to the next visit on June 6. Chris always filled out a form at the doctor's office just prior to an appointment, the psychiatrist's way of learning from the patient's point of view how things had progressed, or not, since the last appointment. This is what Chris reported to his psychiatrist that day: *A friend gave me thirteen 20 mg Adderall. I took 40 mg a day for a week. The drug is a wonder drug for me. I need it. It helps me socially. Gets me motivated with life again. Adderall is not the source of hostility. Things have been fairly calm.*

Based on Chris's statement, which was really a confession of his illegal use of a controlled substance that was not prescribed for him, the psychiatrist prescribed Adderall XR 30 mg, writing in his notes, "To support strength of good IQ to cope." This part of Chris's medical record, which I have copies of, infuriates me to this day. In addition to the comment about support of Chris's IQ, the psychiatrist also noted that Chris's affect was blunted and that he still had ideas of people talking about him and had anger when others intruded on him. Sounded like psychosis to me—delusions and paranoia coupled with the potential for angry, acting-out behavior. Why, why did the psychiatrist not process his own professional observations and assessment of Chris and make a more medically safe decision? Why did he stand by Chris's judgment and ignore the recommendation of the hospital psychiatrists? Why did he discount my reports of the hostility and threatening behavior we saw daily at home?

Why, why did the psychiatrist not process his own professional observations and assessment of Chris and make a more medically safe decision?

Following the early June appointment and Chris's first prescription of Adderall in six months, I wrote my fourth and last letter, telling the psychiatrist about the hospital and home-care stays and Chris's recent behavior at home. In the June 20 letter, I related our serious safety concerns regarding Chris's mental illness. These were our concerns:

June 20, 2005

He has thrown his meds at me and ordered me to pick them up if I expect him to take them. I think he took them today because I told him that he will end up in the hospital if he does not take the meds. He really hates taking them. Chris's anger is seething just under the surface. He pushed his grandfather (age 83) yesterday in a sort of bullheaded manner because he was standing in Chris's pathway . . . On Wednesday of last week, he spoke continually to himself under his breath, like he was muttering. He told me the other people in the room could hear him just fine. Only Chris and I were at home at the time . . . Although he was unhappy about the personal care home placement, he would talk and visit with us in a civil, even pleasant manner (when we went out to eat together) . . . In summary, Chris's explosive tension is a constant concern. His thinking is so delusional that all conversations go one way, with him determined to convince us that his life was ruined when he was baptized, that we never loved him or cared for him, and that we hate him . . . Chris is a time bomb.

I faxed the above letter three days before the appointment. On June 23 Rob took Chris to his appointment and sat with him and the psychiatrist during the session. As usual the session was brief, its purpose being medication management. The primary topics were Chris's request for another Adderall prescription and how life at home was going. Since Adderall is a controlled substance, a new prescription is required each time it is filled. No refills of previous prescriptions are allowed, and the new prescription must be filled by the pharmacy within seven days, or it becomes null and void. When Rob returned home, he was frustrated and angry at the doctor, not only for writing a new prescription for Adderall, but also for his cavalier comments that Chris should stop fighting with his mother. The doctor had said, “Don’t make me get egg on my face,” knowing that we did not want Chris to take that medication. When Rob told me about the session, he said he resented the egg comment because he had been the one with blood on his face in the April altercation with Chris that had led to Chris’s court-ordered hospitalization.

Despite the legal restrictions on writing Adderall prescriptions, the doctor wrote a postdated prescription during that June 23 appointment. He dated the prescription “7/5/05.” We never had a chance to fill it. I found the original prescription in Rob’s wallet several days after he died as a result of Chris’s psychotic rage on June 29, 2005, the day our roller coaster flew off the tracks and crashed.

Part Four

MY NEXT JOURNEY

15

Three Systems to Learn

Following Chris's court arraignment on June 30, 2005, I started on a new course, moving down a learning path which I knew little to nothing about. It was exclusively a train-as-you-go experience. I had no mentor along the way to give me tips or suggestions on which direction I should go. But I did pray boldly and fervently to God, and I thank Him today for His wisdom in providing me with supportive friends and family to go along this path with me. The three systems I had to learn about were the judicial, state mental hospital, and criminal justice systems. This part of the journey lasted six and one-half years and finally took a new direction when Chris's trial was held on November 22, 2011. It was a bench trial, with the judge hearing all testimony and making the ruling. There was no jury. Chris was found "not guilty by reason of insanity." A speedy trial had not been in the cards for my son, but I am thankful for the outcome.

The Harris County Criminal Justice Center, the main courthouse for criminal cases, marked my home base for the judicial system. There are at least four major courthouses in a two-to-three block area in that old part of downtown Houston, which was about twenty-five miles from home and was foreign territory for me. I have received notices for jury service perhaps two times in all the years I have lived in Houston, but I was never picked for a panel. Rob and his mother frequently got jury notices, and each had been chosen to serve on juries. It had been years since I had made any trips downtown.

On my trips to court for Chris's hearings, I always encountered lots of construction, lane blockages, and foot traffic as well as car and bus traffic surrounding those busy buildings. Being unfamiliar with street names and the fact that all were one-way streets made it difficult to feel confident driving downtown in the fourth-largest city in the United States. Except for Chris's first two court hearings, I attended every hearing in Harris County District Court 263 concerning his case. I never saw Chris at any of these hearings, but he was always present in a holding cell next to the courtroom in case his lawyer, the prosecutor, or the judge needed to talk to him. On the day of a hearing, inmates whose cases are on a judge's docket are transported from jail to the Inmate Processing Center. This center is located next to the courthouse, and inmates are transferred for hearings or trials via an underground tunnel that connects the two buildings.

I knew a little more about the state hospital system than the judicial system because of Chris's stay in Rusk State Hospital in 2002. However, the hospital I would soon get to know was North Texas State Hospital, Vernon Campus, usually referred to as Vernon State Hospital, its name before Vernon and another nearby state hospital in Wichita Falls were unified into one administrative entity. Vernon, Texas, is located about thirty miles from the Texas-Oklahoma border and is just across the Red River from my birthplace, Altus, Oklahoma. It is an eight-hour drive from my home in Houston.

When Chris was at Vernon, I went to visit him approximately every six months, usually June and December. For the first visit in December 2005, I drove by myself. I left after work on a Friday afternoon and drove straight through for eight hours. This was not smart. By the time I got within fifty miles of Vernon, I had the car radio blasting and was singing along with Christmas carols at the top of my lungs. I was so exhausted I could barely stay awake. I found a Sonic Drive-In that was still open that late at night and made a quick rest stop before completing the trip. I checked in at a Best Western motel in Vernon, having made advance reservations for late arrival. I made that first trip less than six months after Rob died. I learned a lot on that road trip, mainly that only God could have ensured my safe arrival. I give no credit to my own judgment or decision-making abilities. Altogether, Chris spent thirty-eight months in two separate hospitalizations at Vernon State Hospital. Achieving competency was an elusive goal for him and the hospital staff.

My bull's-eye for the criminal justice system was the 1200 Baker Street jail. There are four county jails in downtown Houston, all in the same vicinity as the district courthouse. I also went to see Chris in jail. I can't say that these occasions were really visits; the jail environment almost totally prevented any meaningful communication. The best I can say is that I got to see Chris, and he got to see me. But eventually he stopped responding to the call that he had a visitor, and I did not see him on many of my visits at the jail. I did not understand at the time, but I do now. Because of his extreme psychotic state, he was unable as well as unwilling to leave his solitary cell. I went alone only one time to see him at the jail. Otherwise, my brother Steve or Will always went with me. I would not allow my female friends or female family members to go with me. When I visited Chris in jail, I always felt as if I had entered a black hole in an unknown universe. Because of competency issues, Chris was transferred back and forth between jail and the hospital. He had three stays in jail with two lengthy hospitalizations in between. The first of his three stays in jail lasted four months; then he was transferred to Vernon State Hospital. Chris was incarcerated a total of forty months in Baker Street jail. The criminal justice system was the most closed of the three systems in terms of being transparent about its operations.

There was a fourth subsystem that interfaced closely with all three of the systems. This was the Harris County Mental Health and Mental Retardation Authority (MHMRA). The judges in the judicial system gave MHMRA orders to evaluate inmates. MHMRA is the local arm of the Division for Mental Health and Substance Abuse Services, Texas Department of State Health

Services, which also governs state mental hospitals. The staff of MHMRA's forensic unit had offices at the 1200 Baker Street jail. This was where MHMRA's competency and sanity evaluations of Chris were conducted.

The three major systems had some common elements, in addition to the connection with MHMRA, and for the most part they successfully communicated with each other. However, all three are major bureaucratic structures with their own peculiarities and cultures. Each was also subject to budget constraints and political vagaries. Trying to understand each system and get what I needed to know took patience and constant attention to Chris's circumstances. I had absolutely no control, but I observed, asked questions, and when possible, offered clarification to lawyers and hospital staff. It quickly became clear to me that for these three systems, I was the expert on our past and knew Chris's illness better than anyone other than Chris himself. However, that did not mean I was sought out for what I might contribute. Over time I built relationships with court administrators, bailiffs, MHMRA caseworkers, hospital social workers, and the courthouse parking-lot attendant, who would let me know if some media-grabbing event was happening downtown. A lot goes on in the Harris County Criminal Justice Center that makes the news, and I wanted no part of that.

> I had absolutely had no control, but I observed, asked questions, and when possible, offered clarification to lawyers and hospital staff.

16

The Judicial System

Chris was arraigned in Harris County District Court 263 before Judge Jim Wallace, who has maintained control of Chris's case from the first arraignment until now. I did not attend the arraignment hearing because I was recuperating from the assault the day before and was emotionally and mentally numb from the results of Chris's attack on his father and me. Steve attended the court hearing in my place. Steve met Chris's court-appointed lawyer, who had little to tell Steve. He had just met Chris in the courtroom's holding cell a few minutes before he stood with Chris to make a plea before the judge. The lawyer explained the process of requesting a psych evaluation to determine competency to stand trial due to Chris's history of treatment for mental illness. He would make a motion to the court and was confident that the judge would grant the request. That was the lawyer's job to do, not mine. The family had no say in any of this process. If Steve had not approached the attorney to introduce himself, I doubt that we would have known anything about the next step for Chris.

My sister-in-law, Patty, called a distant family member who was a criminal attorney for advice. He told her to use the court-appointed attorney because we could never afford the expense of hiring our own lawyer. He encouraged her to trust the Harris County system of court-appointed representation for indigent individuals. He was right in his recommendation. The first attorney Steve met with was on board when the judge granted the initial motion for the determination of "competency to stand trial" and continued as the attorney of record during Chris's first four months in jail. Later the judge appointed another attorney who represented Chris for the remainder of his criminal case.

It took almost four months to comply with the judicial order to determine competency. Since MHMRA was in charge of this aspect of the case, a staff psychologist, who would administer the evaluation protocol, had to be scheduled.

Next, Chris's evaluation was completed, and finally a report was written and submitted to the judge, Chris's attorney, and the prosecutor who was the assistant district attorney (ADA) assigned to Judge Wallace's court. Each party had to review the psychologist's report with his recommendation and assessment of Chris's competency. After this step a hearing was placed on the court's docket for the judge to hear from the defense and state and then make his ruling. I was present in the courtroom and heard the judge rule that Chris was not competent and then heard the judge order his transfer to a state hospital for treatment. I did not know what that meant but felt confident that everyone was getting the idea that Chris was truly mentally ill.

When I first started going to Chris's hearings, I felt intimidated by the drive downtown and an 8:00 a.m. arrival time. I soon learned that 8:00 a.m. did not apply to me because I was only an observer in court. But I did need to arrive by 10:00 to make sure I did not miss anything that involved Chris. I worried about where to park but found a parking lot one block from the courthouse and parked there every time I went to the courthouse for a hearing. Usually I paid ten dollars to park, but sometimes I paid fifteen if the Astros were playing a game that day or five if I arrived after 10:00 a.m. If traffic was especially bad and the lot was full, I would ask the attendant what was going on. He would tell me if a major case was being decided in court and if the media were all around. From this I would know that the line waiting to pass through the metal detectors in the courthouse would be slow and all the elevators would be full. I felt more prepared to enter the courthouse environment when I knew what was going on.

I would pass the same two panhandlers on the street every time I went to court. After a while I became more comfortable just walking past them, as most other people did.

In the courtroom itself I began to recognize the same players every time I went. Not only was there the same judge, but there were also the same assistant district attorneys, same court-appointed lawyers, same bailiffs, and same court clerks and administrative staff. There was always a small audience in the courtroom. I rarely spoke to anyone but figured out they were either in court for their own case or for a family member's case. I watched as individuals were called before the judge with their attorneys standing beside them. Sometimes the person had been released on bail and was in court to hear the judge rule on an investigative report or probation evaluation. I also witnessed individuals who had recently been arrested and were being brought before the judge for an arraignment. Wearing orange jail jumpsuits, they were ushered in wearing handcuffs before the judge, who heard each person's plea and then gave his ruling.

When I saw the television news clip of Chris as he first stood before the judge at his arraignment, I noticed he was wearing an orange inmate uniform that had "MED" stamped on the back. I thought it stood for "medical unit" and felt a sense of relief; surely now Chris would be given his medication. This ended up being a wrong conclusion, which I figured out after a few more court and jail visits. "MED" stood for "medium," as in small, medium, and large.

Rarely was a family member able to talk to a defendant after his case was called by the judge for arraignment or sentencing. I saw this happen only one time with a young man who had failed to comply with his probation order. The judge revoked his probation and ordered him to prison immediately. The young man was allowed to give his sobbing family member his wallet and belt before being taken away in handcuffs by the bailiff. I also saw three jury trials on my days in court when I had come for one of Chris's hearings. They were about two hours in duration.

There were actually two reasons I went to court for every hearing. The first reason was I wanted to be present if something unexpected was decided. The second reason became the more important reason. I began to view this time as my appointment with Chris's attorney. He was always in court if Chris's case was on the docket. He would tell me what he was doing on the case and inform me of conversations he had had with the judge or the prosecutor. He gave me copies of documents pertaining to the case, including copies of the psychologist's reports and the judge's recommendations. I was able to tell him things I knew about Chris's history and let him know what Chris was telling me about his symptoms when he became suicidal in jail. I had long known that Chris felt compelled to keep his thoughts from the government telepaths. This included just about everyone in the judicial, state hospital, and criminal justice systems. He believed that his attorney was an agent of the government and for a long time would not converse with him.

I began to view this time as my appointment with Chris's attorney.

Another benefit I soon realized was that I was viewed as one of Chris's victims by the prosecutors. They would introduce themselves to me and also tell me how the case was progressing. I had one long interview with the first assistant DA assigned as the prosecutor for Chris's case. We met privately in an interview room outside the courtroom on one of my hearing visits. I had no idea in advance that this would happen. It was an emotional conversation because he took me through the entire event of June 29, 2005, and asked many questions about Chris's prior years of treatment for mental illness. He had a fat folder that held all the documents for the case. He also had a large envelope of Rob's autopsy photographs. He took notes while I talked. He explained some of the politics commonly known about Harris County's hard-line approach regarding mental illness cases. This was not news to me, but it was very distressing to hear it from an insider of the DA's office. Rarely were defendants that claimed mental illness or *insanity*, the legal term, ever found not guilty. He told me that Chris's case was the strongest he had ever seen for an insanity plea. He expressed empathy for what my family had been through for so long. He seemed to understand that I had lost both my husband and my son that day in June. Then he said, however, that he was the "only liberal" in the DA's office and that he was about to be transferred to a new job. He agreed to write a comprehensive report of his interview with me and include his recommendations for how to pursue Chris's case. He also said he would talk to the supervising prosecutor about the case and would make a recommendation for which assistant DA should follow up when he was transferred to his new job.

Toward the end of the interview with the prosecutor, I asked him if he was wise . . . I said that I hoped he would be the rainbow for Chris.

Despite all the stress and worry whirling around inside me, I felt bold that morning. I had seen a rainbow on my way to downtown, and it had brightened my spirits. I knew God had put that rainbow in the sky to bring me comfort, and I prayed to God to give me His wisdom as I entered the courthouse that morning, not knowing I would be facing a difficult conversation with the prosecutor in Chris's case. Toward the end of the interview with the prosecutor, I asked him if he was wise. He looked puzzled and did not know what to say to me. Then I told him about the rainbow and what it had meant to me. I said that I hoped he would be the rainbow for Chris.

When I left the courthouse and went to my car, I sat inside and sobbed for a long time. Then I went home and slept for two hours.

One other thing I learned about prosecutors through my court attendance is that they are frequently moved around to different courts. This turned out to be a cause of many delays. A new prosecutor meant that he or she had to get up to speed on all the cases in Court 263, and many hearings would be rescheduled. Occasionally I went to court only to learn that the hearing had been postponed and a new date entered on the docket. Of course, no one told me that when I first arrived in the courtroom. I would wait for up to an hour, and then I would ask if Chris's attorney was present. That's when the bailiff would tell me that Chris's case had been reset, and the court administrator would give me the new date. Often the new date was a full month away.

From observing all the activity in the courtroom on the judge's side of the gate, I decided that this was really just an office for all persons present doing business before the judge. They had casual conversations among themselves, made personal phone calls, did business with the other side—defense spoke with prosecution, met with clients, completed paperwork, and worked on their computers. They were not particularly quiet except when the judge was on the bench. He came and left the bench regularly throughout the morning. Unless there were pleas to be heard, a motion to hear or grant, or a trial in progress, the judge would leave the bench. I saw him wear traditional black robes only when he was giving directions to a jury pool prior to being interviewed by the lawyers for possible selection to serve on a jury for an upcoming case in his court.

With my regular visits to Chris's hearings, I eventually overcame my intimidation about being in the courtroom. I learned that if I needed the bailiff's attention in order to ask a question, I could stand quietly at the gate and wait for him to come over to me and ask what I needed. If my question could be answered only by the court administrator, he opened the gate and she would call me over. After a time they came to recognize me, and they knew who and where Chris's attorney was without my having to say his name. One lunchtime, when everyone was asked to vacate the courtroom, the bailiff motioned for me to stay because he knew I was still waiting for Chris's attorney, who was in a trial that morning in another courtroom. I was allowed to stay through lunch and until Chris's attorney arrived, but I could not have food. No food, drinks, gum, shorts, newspapers, or ringing cell phones were allowed in District Court 263.

17

The State Mental Health Hospital System

In Texas mental health services for individuals without insurance, including inpatient treatment in state mental hospitals, fall under the auspices of the Texas Department of State Health Services (TDSHS). This is a very large state agency that touches the lives of all Texas residents in many ways. The Mental Health and Substance Abuse Services division is one of five major divisions in TDSHS. The other divisions include Family and Community Health Services, Disease Control and Prevention Services, Regional and Local Health Services, and Regulatory Services. There are eight state mental hospitals and three smaller mental health centers located across Texas. Of the three systems I was involved with, this one is the largest and most complex. However, it was also the one system I was familiar with, partly because of Chris's many hospitalizations and my training as a counselor.

North Texas State Hospital is made up of two campuses: one in Wichita Falls and one in Vernon. They are about fifty miles apart, and some of the professional staff work at both facilities. The Vernon Campus is the maximum-security hospital for patients like Chris, persons with a severe mental illness who are also charged with a serious crime. It provides forensic services for the entire state of Texas, offering both a 284-bed maximum security program for adults and a 78-bed adolescent forensic program for dually diagnosed (mental illness and substance abuse) thirteen- to seventeen-year-olds who are involved with the juvenile justice system. The Wichita Falls Campus provides general psychiatric inpatient services for child, adolescent, adult, and geriatric patients with a bed capacity of 330. Before Vernon became the center for all court-involved persons with a mental illness, it was a general psychiatric hospital serving thirty counties in the far North Texas region.

First Stay in Vernon State Hospital

Because my first visit to Vernon was in December, the area looked mostly brown and tan—and desolate. This part of Texas consists of acres and acres of farm and ranch land with pumping oil wells scattered across the flat terrain. Eighteen-wheel trucks are the primary traffic along this lengthy, straight highway heading west. The drive allows for a lot of thinking and reflecting time. After my first trip I asked either Steve or Will to go with me. That was a much better way to handle the time and strain of the trip. I could think and reflect out loud and had the benefit of their feedback, which was usually that I was too hard on myself, I had done the best I could, and Chris's illness was not my fault. I needed to hear those words to stay encouraged and to keep going. My cotravelers gave me practical, emotional, and spiritual support on my visits to see Chris. It was not an easy or convenient trip for them to make. Their willingness to interrupt their own busy lives to make that dreary, stressful ride up the road to North Texas blessed me, and I am so grateful to have had those wonderful men standing beside me, helping me take one step, or mile, at a time.

When I visited Chris at Vernon, I'd go through a security check and could not take in a camera or cell phone or anything that could be dangerous. Whatever I brought to give Chris was opened and inventoried by the security guards. I could not bring food, hardback books, pens or pencils, composition books with wire binding, shoes with laces, belts, or anything bulky. Food brought in ants. Hardback books, pens and pencils, and wire from composition books could all be used as a weapon. Laces and belts could result in harm to self or others. Storage was limited, so choices of clothing were minimally allowed. I got used to bringing Chris's coats and sweaters home at the June visit and to taking them back to him at the December visit. North Texas seasons are definitely not like Houston's, where we have less variability and can wear lightweight clothing almost year-round. Vernon had cold, windy winters and hot, windy summers. Spring and fall provided nice transitions to Vernon's serious seasonal changes.

The first time I saw Chris at Vernon, he looked sick. What does that mean to you, my reader? Please try to visualize this image. His dark, curly hair was long, wild, and thinning. His appearance was unkempt. His eyes were dark and darting. He trembled and yet sat rigidly in a straight-backed chair. He had no facial expression other than anxiety. He looked like someone your children would fear and someone you would want to keep at a distance yourself. In short, he looked mentally ill and potentially dangerous, whether to me or to himself I could not say.

He looked like someone your children would fear and someone you would want to keep at a distance yourself.

There was a heavy wire screen from the countertop to the ceiling that stretched between us. We were the only two in the visiting area although there were places for six people on my side. I leaned in closely to talk to him because he spoke so softly I could hardly hear him.

This first visit was difficult. I was wary of saying the wrong thing or seeming to pry into his thoughts. I was waiting for him to give me a lead in a conversation, but that did not happen. I told him I was glad to see him and I hoped he was doing okay. He stared back at me. After a few minutes of my fumbling and smiling, he told me the guards were listening. I did not think so and tried to reassure him. Then he looked over my shoulder at a wall and said, "There. Didn't you hear him laughing?" I knew he was psychotic and hallucinating, and the same paranoid delusions were running amok in his mind. He said he wanted to go back to his unit, so I told the guard that the visit was finished. Chris waited while a unit staff member came to get him and escorted him back. At least he was not handcuffed as he had been when I saw him the first time in jail.

After our less-than-fifteen-minute visit, I was able to meet with Chris's social worker. I had spoken on the phone with her a few times before the visit and was anxious to meet her face to face. Chris was still in the competency unit, where all the treatment was intended to get him competent to stand trial. It had been one month since he had been found "not competent to stand trial" and was admitted to Vernon on the judge's ninety-day order to receive treatment. The social worker explained this process to me, letting me know that the hospital would advise the judge on Chris's progress and likely would request an extension on the court order for hospitalization. She did not expect any real progress for Chris without long-term treatment. As yet, the medication did not appear to be stabilizing him. He was having frequent hostile interactions and fights with other patients and staff. At other times the reverse would happen, with him staying in bed all day, not going to class or group meetings, and refusing to take showers and eat meals. I told her how Chris and his former therapist used to walk around outside during his therapy sessions. She said she would try this approach to building a relationship with him informally. A few weeks later she called me with an update on Chris and told me this approach had worked and he had begun to show some trust and willingness to talk to her. She would go outside to meet up with him when she saw him on the grounds pacing back and forth. Score one for Mom's input!

The social worker was kind and encouraged me to be patient with the patient! On this first visit she took me on a tour of the hospital grounds and buildings, except for the residential units. I saw their general activity and snack-bar area known as the canteen, vocational training areas, a gym, classrooms, including one set up like a courtroom, and a large auditorium. I don't think Chris had seen those areas yet because all the patients were on a token behavioral system and earned visits to those areas as rewards for meeting weekly goals. As long as Chris refused to go to class or take showers or was getting into fights, he stayed on a "white card," meaning no trips out of his unit. He did have access to a large activity room and a small, fenced yard area that was part of the unit.

The social worker told me Chris rarely left his room, and when he did come out, he was often agitated about something or someone, which would lead to hostile interactions such as cursing, threatening, or fighting. He hated the TV and always thought it was loudly talking about him and making fun of him. He also accused anyone who was loud or laughing of mocking and taunting him. This included both staff and patients. Additionally, he would refuse to take his medication at times.

Chris's first stay at Vernon lasted twenty-one months. The social worker's instinct about his progress was absolutely correct. He continued to slide into psychosis and stayed there. Every six months the Dangerousness Review Board met to assess Chris. This is a required evaluation of every patient in the mental health forensic unit. The review board is made up of mental health professionals who are on staff at other state mental hospitals. The individuals whom the board reviews are not patients of anyone who serves on the review board. The Vernon hospital staff submits reports and psychiatric evaluations on each patient, and the patient appears before the board to be interviewed. I received a letter every six months inviting me to attend the review board meeting and provide testimony. The social worker also called me in advance of the hearings to tell me what the hospital's recommendation would be. I learned to trust the process and never attended one of the review board meetings. The hospital knew Chris's condition better than I did at that point, and they operated in the best interest of Chris, his victim pool (Will, Seth, and me), and the public.

> The hospital knew Chris's condition better than I did at that point.

As long as he was psychotic, paranoid, and delusional, Chris was unpredictable and presented a danger to himself and others.

I visited Chris at Vernon a total of five times during this twenty-one-month period. The social worker called me approximately every two months to update me on Chris's progress. She was able to do that because Chris had signed the authorization form allowing her to share information with me. Chris also called about once a month and wrote periodic letters. I didn't know what he knew or remembered about the events of June 29, 2005. I didn't talk to Chris about the criminal case because I was fearful of saying something that might impact the case and trial that was before him. In those first few months, I knew so little about the judicial system that I felt captive, almost as if I were a prisoner too. Was a prison sentence just around the corner, in ninety days or less? Was Chris still so suicidal that he might try to kill himself? Would his serious mental illness be recognized for its role in Rob's death? I could not picture any future for me that I thought I could survive, much less one that Chris might survive. That was my lowest point along the road of Chris's mental illness following Rob's death.

My next three visits to Chris all played out much like the first one. He was still quiet and leery of my presence and the world around him. Though guarded, he seemed pleased with the books and personal items I brought him. My gifts became the topic of our conversations as we sat across from each other with the screen separating us. Our conversations gradually became more coherent and two way, with better eye contact. Over time he started attending classes, taking showers, and generally being cooperative with staff requests. I knew he was getting better and could tell that his thinking was clearer. With the progress he had made in the almost-two years at Vernon, I was not surprised when Chris called me the night before he was to be transported back to Harris County to tell me he had been found competent to stand trial. I felt ambivalent upon hearing his news—glad he was better, but scared he would be thrown into the jail environment that had been so harmful to him previously. During this phone call he didn't want to tell me any details of how he was doing because he said the phones were tapped and "they" were listening in. When I got off the phone, I seriously doubted that Chris was really competent, but I had no control in the matter. So I just prayed for his safe travel.

Second Stay in Vernon State Hospital

The competent state of mind did not last long after Chris returned to Harris County jail. Within seven months he was sent back to Vernon State Hospital, having been found not competent to stand trial during a December psychological evaluation. That time he stayed at Vernon for seventeen months during 2008 and 2009. I made three visits to see him during that hospital stay. There, he finally began to make progress. He became less aggressive and didn't get into fights. He also made progress on the card system—earning privileges for the first time, like being allowed to walk around outside his unit or buy a soft drink and candy bar at the canteen. He earned the opportunity to have a job in his unit, for which he was paid minimum wage. We began to plan my visits together, with him asking me to bring certain things and my asking him to clear the visit with the social worker. He would do it, and she would call me when she had the psychiatrist's approval. It was a good sign that Chris was able to take some responsibility for his own life by setting up our visits. The improvement was likely due to a new medication, Clozaril, which Chris began to take shortly after returning to Vernon in 2008. It took more than a year for his stabilized condition to look real. Ultimately, Chris was again deemed competent to stand trial by the hospital, and the judge ordered his return to Harris County jail in August 2009. More than four years had passed since Rob was killed. The Harris County judicial system would take another two years before deciding that Chris had been legally mentally ill—insane—on June 29, 2005.

18

The Criminal Justice System

The Baker Street jail houses special populations of inmates, including those who are mentally ill. Because of Chris's mental illness history, he was jailed at the facility where MHMRA, the county arm of the Texas state hospital division of the state health department, had staff. This was where Chris was when the first psych evaluation was attempted following the judge's order at the second hearing after his arraignment. The mental health staff at the jail makes up the local forensic unit and includes psychiatrists and psychologists who evaluate for competency and sanity. Psychiatrists also prescribe medication and supervise treatment. Nurses administer medication and monitor the status of mentally ill inmates. The jailers in this facility wear uniforms that look more like street clothes than police uniforms, and they receive special training to work with mentally ill prisoners. They are in a position of authority but understand that many of their prisoners hear voices and have chronic delusions. They're trained how to de-escalate potentially explosive situations and can make changes in cell-block assignments if a prisoner is too disruptive.

This happened with Chris once when a new mentally ill inmate who was placed with him continually yelled out and talked to himself night and day. His erratic behavior conflicted with Chris's delusion of telepathy and caused him

Whatever people's purpose, God's will prevailed, and Chris avoided being preyed on or exploited by fellow inmates of the Baker Street jail.

to become agitated, thinking that the man was threatening and insulting him. The two posed a dangerous situation for everyone around them. So a guard moved Chris to a more stable cell block, which allowed him some peace of mind and diminished the risk factors. In another instance an inmate was trying to extort money from Chris to use for his weekly snack purchase. Chris gained the courage to tell a jailer, and this inmate was moved to another floor. I doubt that compassion for the mentally ill was the motivation for assisting Chris; rather, ensuring safety for the inmate population as a whole was the likely reason behind these accommodating decisions by those in charge. Whatever people's purpose, God's will prevailed, and Chris avoided being preyed on or exploited by fellow inmates of the Baker Street jail.

Three Stays in Baker Street Jail

Chris's worst time in jail was the first four months following his arrest. There was no movement on his case because of the judge's order to determine competency. He was not very communicative when I visited him except for my first visit the evening before Rob's funeral. Frequently he did not come out for a visit at all. When he did come out to the visitation area, he looked bedraggled and unkempt and was always handcuffed. Rarely did he say more than one word at a time—"yes," "no," or "okay." He didn't have his glasses and seemed to have no clue where they might be. One time he had a black eye and told me he didn't know how it happened. During the last two months of this first jail stay, Chris didn't come out for any visits at all.

On September 30, 2005, three months into Chris's jail stay, an MHMRA psychologist attempted to complete the clinical interview part of his psych evaluation ordered by Judge Wallace. He reported that when he arrived at

Chris's solitary cell, the psychologist "saw via a small window in his door that he was resting on his bed, and he was covered with a blanket. I knocked on his door twice, but he did not move in his bed or respond in any way." When the deputy arrived momentarily and opened the cell door, Chris raised his head, stared without speaking for "about a minute," and then put his head down again without further interaction. The psychologist asked the jail deputy if Chris was always like this. He acknowledged that it was Chris's usual demeanor and that "on occasion Mr. Malone would smile, but he would not speak." The psychologist stated then that he could not conduct the evaluation because Chris was not competent to understand anything the psychologist was required to discuss with him. The psychologist reported back to the court that Chris was incompetent and recommended that he be admitted to a state mental hospital in order to receive treatment to become competent. When the hearing was held, I was present in court. The judge ordered Chris to be transferred to North Texas State Hospital, Vernon Campus.

It was almost two years later before the Vernon social worker shared the full details of Chris's condition during that first attempted evaluation. That's when I truly understood the mighty power of a horrific psychotic state and what it could do to completely dehumanize a person.

That's when I truly understood the mighty power of a horrific psychotic state and what it could do to completely dehumanize a person.

Chris's second period of incarceration lasted seven months, July 2007 through January 2008. The transition back to jail from the hospital went much smoother than when he was jailed following his arrest. The hospital had sent a two-week supply of his medication so he could stay on it as prescribed, allowing MHMRA time to get Chris back into their system. A discharge summary was also sent to inform the MHMRA treatment team of his most recent progress. Nevertheless, Chris's condition deteriorated in a short time. My theory is, the change itself caused a setback, and the jail stress level is so much greater than that at the hospital. I also do not think Chris was yet stable enough to leave the hospital, based on his paranoid and delusional comments to me the night before his transfer.

From my point of view, Chris's third and last stay at Baker Street jail, lasting twenty-eight months, was the longest and most frustrating. Inmates enjoyed no activity time other than a twenty-four-hour TV playing in a large communal room in the middle of the cell blocks. Chris's only look at the sky or outside world was during the five-minute bus ride from his jail to the Inmate Processing Center next door to the courthouse on his hearing days. During his last incarceration, Chris and I agreed I would not come for visits because the conditions were so poor. Instead, he called me collect about every ten days, and we talked about how the two of us were doing. My phone bill jumped about fifty dollars a month because of the collect-call expense.

One reason for the lengthy, two-year-plus stay was the continual postponements in Court 263. The judge had surgery, a new district attorney was elected, and many changes occurred in prosecutors' court assignments. In September 2009, six weeks after Chris's return to jail as competent, MHMRA filed a three-page evaluation report saying Chris was sane at the time of Rob's stabbing. Chris's attorney was shocked and told me he wanted another opinion. He then filed motions for an independent psychiatric evaluation. The trial was reset many times. Even after an independent psych evaluation was completed and filed with the court on October 3, 2010, the trial was not held for thirteen more months.

The state decided it wanted another opinion from an MHMRA psychologist since the defense and state evaluations had such widely different conclusions. Months passed while motions about selecting and paying the doctor and determining the scope of the evaluation flew between the state and defense attorneys.

A third MHMRA sanity evaluation was conducted a few months before Chris's trial was finally held on November 22, 2011, with testimony heard regarding three MHMRA evaluations and one independent evaluation.

Visiting Chris in Jail

When I visited Chris in jail during his first and second stays at Baker Street, I had to fill out a form with his unique numbers that identified his jail site and his cell block. I had to give this form along with my driver's license to a deputy before passing through a metal detector. Along with my driver's license, I could have only one key in my possession, not my car keys on a ring, but one car key. No purse, no cell phone, no umbrella. I had to stand in long lines for each step in this process—completing the form, talking with the deputy, and passing through the metal detector. This process often took more than an hour. Finally I reached the elevator and pushed the button to the second floor.

One time I saw two volunteers from a local church manning the forms table and helping people. Very few visitors knew their inmates' ID numbers when they came to visit, which meant they had to look up the names in a huge book of printouts where every inmate in any Harris County jail was listed. Rarely were visitor-request forms or pencils to be found on the table. Then it was always a hassle to complete the form. So these women were like angels! They had forms. They had pencils. They explained how to use the book to get the information everyone needed. These volunteers provided the only bright spot I ever saw in that building. They smiled, spoke respectfully, and were helpful without intruding. Not just to me but to everyone. I said a little prayer that they would be safe, and I thanked them for their service and helpfulness.

When I arrived at the floor designated for my visit, I had to pass my form through a slot in a dark window. No one spoke to me, but I knew there was a person on the other side of the window because the form was taken. There were no signs to tell a person what to do or where to go when you stepped off the elevator. I sympathized with those bewildered-looking, first-time visitors, who reminded me of my first visit. But I never spoke with another visitor, nor did anyone ever speak to me.

Some visitors brought young children, which really bothered me. The sounds of crying babies were added to the loud, angry, and often profane language I heard among visitors and inmates. I didn't like for the children to be exposed to this raw side of humanity. One time I redirected a young boy back to his parents, who were standing near the elevator. While they were trying to figure out what to do, their child started wandering down the hall into the ugliness of the visitation area. When a loud stream of profanity burst out, I quickly put my hands over his ears, smiled at him, and gently guided him back to his parents. He appeared to be about eight years old, the same age as my grandson, and my heart ached.

19

The Trial

On November 22, 2011, Chris's trial was finally held. I was told to be in court early that morning since his case would probably come up first on the docket. I received this information the day before in a phone call from the secretary of Chris's attorney. I had been expecting to hear that another delay had occurred and felt almost surprised that the trial might actually take place. Should I prepare, review any notes, or check dates of certain events? The secretary told me the psychiatrist would do the testifying; I just needed to be present.

Will took off from work, and he went with me downtown. I was so focused on the experience before me that I could barely hold a conversation with him during the twenty-five-mile drive to the courthouse. It took an hour to reach our destination. We left Will's house at peak morning rush hour on that gray, rainy day. Traffic was slow, and I struggled with my frustration of wanting to hurry. But patience was a lesson I had learned well from 2005 to 2011. I prayed that God would be with me, the judge, the attorneys, and, most of all, Chris. My faith told me God was present, and I gradually let go of the anxiety I had felt since the law secretary's phone call.

We entered the courtroom early enough, although it was later than I had planned before I discovered we would have a wet freeway commute. I led us to my usual bench, off to the left side of the visitors' area near the front where I liked to sit during my court visits. It was a small bench, but we crowded in together, and it felt good to be physically close and touching someone I knew loved and cared about me. I shared with Will my knowledge about the people and process on the judge's side of the gate. I'm sure this was mostly nervous chatter on my part, and I don't know if Will was even listening to me. The judge was not in the courtroom, and attorneys were getting set for the day, talking among themselves or to the court clerks and bailiffs, taking and making phone calls on their cell phones, or going to and from the next-door holding cell area. A small group of individuals with court business were sitting in the visitors' section where we were. People continued to stream in and take a seat. I did not know it at the time, but the state's witness in Chris's case, an MHMRA psychologist, was sitting in the row behind us. I did not see Chris's attorney or the independent psychiatrist who would testify on the defense side.

When she asked to speak to me privately before the trial started, red flags shot up.

In a few moments the prosecutor came over and introduced herself to us. When she asked to speak to me privately before the trial started, red flags shot up. I asked if Will could come with me, and she said yes. I felt so protective of Chris. I was still ambivalent about what the outcome should, would, or could be. Bottom line, I was totally convinced in both heart and head that Chris was very sick with a mental illness that he had lived with for sixteen years, which now at age thirty was over half of his lifetime. The disease had stripped him of courage, initiative, confidence, his quick wit and clever sense of humor, his tenderheartedness, his strong will and determination to figure problems out on his own, and even his good looks. Saddest of all, Chris had lost trust in everything and everyone in heaven and on earth.

When Will and I sat down in the interview room with the prosecutor, she told me she would be calling me as a witness for the state. I asked her what that meant, and she told me she would ask me to review the day of Rob's death for the court. Anxious thoughts flew into my mind. I knew it; I should have done some homework last night! No one had told me I would be a witness for the prosecution!

But as I listened silently to the prosecutor explain what questions she would ask, God's peace exuded out my pores. I knew He had equipped me for every good work, and finally getting to tell the truth about that day was a good work. Telling the truth is always a good work. I felt confident and unafraid. I was composed and asked the prosecutor a few questions so I could fully understand the testifying procedure. Chris's attorney had never spoken to me about testifying.

> Saddest of all, Chris had lost trust in everything and everyone in heaven and on earth.

Finally, the prosecutor told me she would show me a picture of Rob and would ask me to identify him for the court record when I was on the stand. "Fine, no problem," I replied. Then she said she had an autopsy picture of Rob and she wanted to show it to me before I was on the witness stand. Will and I both felt stunned. We looked incredulously at her and each other. I tentatively said okay. She had held the photograph in her lap facedown the whole time we had talked, and I had not noticed it. She then handed the picture to me. I looked at it and took a deep breath. My first comment was that it did not look like Rob. It was an upper body and head shot showing the lifeless form of a man with a long scar running from his neck to below his waistline. It looked like a seam line to me. I had to stare at the photograph quietly for a few moments to search for any resemblance to my funny, lively, sweet husband. I then asked if I could show it to Will, and she said yes. With strong emotion softening his voice, Will said, "Oh, Mom." I knew he was experiencing a sense of disbelief. We had previously seen his dad in death two times together—at the hospital and the funeral—and now in this photograph. Never did any view we saw of Rob following June 29, 2005, look like who he really was in life. Only the loving, living husband and father occupies a permanent place in our hearts and memories.

The sadness, pain, and shock of that day more than six years before rushed back as if they were current, here-and-now feelings.

What had just happened to us was a lot for Will and me to process. The sadness, pain, and shock of that day more than six years before rushed back as if they were current, here-and-now feelings. But they were old feelings, six-and-a-half-year-old feelings, in fact. How could my feelings do that to me? How could they cause me to feel weak and shaky and dizzy like this? I remember thinking about the joy I felt when Will arrived that afternoon at the emergency room, how big and strong he looked, how relieved I felt that he had finally made it safely home to be by my side. I realized I was feeling the same sense of relief and thankfulness with him sitting next to me in court. How could I feel so blessed and so sorrowful at the same time?

These were questions I was asking myself fifteen minutes before Chris's trial was to begin. I grasped that the answers were beyond my wisdom, and I drew myself back from this train of thought. The reality of the moment was, Will and I were in court for Chris's trial. It was November 22, 2011, not June 29, 2005, even if just a few minutes before it had felt like it. I started to look around the courtroom, checking out my surroundings, and a peace came over me again. I felt calm as I watched Chris being escorted in by the bailiff through the holding-cell doorway.

By now his attorney sat in place at the defense table. They each smiled at me, and I smiled and nodded back at them. Chris was wearing an inmate's orange jumpsuit. I was told he did not need street clothes because no jury would be present, but I wished he could have worn his own clothing. This day was hugely important in Chris's life. He looked neat, was clean shaven, and had his hair cut short. I had not seen him face to face in twenty-nine months, since my last visit to Vernon, a month before he was transferred back to Harris County jail.

Shortly after Chris and his attorney took their places at the defense table, the judge entered the courtroom. The bailiff said, "All rise," and we did. And then he said, "You may be seated," and we were. Then the judge called for the first case on the docket, "The State of Texas versus Christopher Allen Malone in the felony charge of murder." Both attorneys responded affirmatively to the judge that they were present and ready to proceed. Next I heard my name called by the prosecutor as the first witness. I touched Chris on the shoulder as I walked past him on my way to the witness stand. This may have violated courtroom protocol, but no one said anything. I stood in front of the witness stand, was sworn in, and took my seat. I still felt calm.

In my job as a counselor, I had been subpoenaed to testify in court in child-abuse and child-custody cases a few times, so I had received training in proper witness demeanor on the stand. I knew to demonstrate a quiet and calm attitude and answer the questions straightforwardly without elaboration. If elaboration was wanted or needed, the examining attorney would ask for it. The real reason for my feeling of calmness was that I had given over to God the care and protection of my family and myself. I could only tell the truth of my story, and the rest was in the hands of God. I knew He was in charge and He would prevail that day. I did not have to understand all that had led to this point in my life. He had an important job for me to do on the stand, and I felt ready. My testimony was for God as well as for Chris and the state of Texas.

Just as the prosecutor was about to ask her first question of me, the judge interrupted her to ask about the wording of the indictment. For the next ten minutes, I sat quietly and watched from the witness stand while Chris's attorney, the prosecutor, and the supervising assistant DA all tried to satisfy the judge's questions. The paperwork before the judge had wording taken from the original indictment and had statements that he wanted clarified. Never bet on how a judge will rule! I momentarily thought the trial was about to be postponed and subsequently felt a new appreciation for Chris's attorney and his past unwillingness to tell me when something new or important might happen in court. There are too many variables to predict a specific outcome.

What a similarity to living with mental illness! You can't predict improvement or disaster. Take one day at a time. Be as prepared as possible. Know that setbacks are part of the journey.

What a similarity to living with mental illness! You can't predict improvement or disaster. Take one day at a time. Be as prepared as possible. Know that setbacks are part of the journey. That was the reality in the courtroom and in my family.

The judge eventually was satisfied that the trial could go forward. The prosecutor began to ask me questions, mostly about my recollection of what happened the day of Rob's stabbing. I answered all of them calmly and as fully as she requested. She finally got to the point of showing me the autopsy photograph for the identification of Rob as the victim. I glanced at the photograph for a very brief moment and handed it back to her. She asked if the person in the picture was my husband, Robert Malone. I said yes.

She then went on to ask me questions about Chris's behavior after the stabbing. It felt as if she was going someplace with these questions, but I didn't know where. After my recovery from blacking out on the kitchen floor, my only memories were about trying to get help for Rob. She asked me if I saw or heard certain things, but I had no knowledge of what she was asking. She repeated those questions in different ways, but I still did not know or remember anything about other events, which she seemed to be referring to, that might have happened that day.

After I spent bout fifteen to twenty minutes with the prosecutor, the defense attorney began questioning me. He began asking me a series of short questions about the long line of psychiatrists, therapists, and hospitals Chris had received treatment from. He asked, "Was Dr. —— a psychiatrist who treated Chris?"

I answered, "Yes."

Then he asked, "Was Dr. —— a psychiatrist who treated Chris?" He continued asking this same question to me, but naming a different doctor with each subsequent question. In the same manner he asked about each hospital and therapist that had treated Chris. When he finished, I had confirmed that Chris had been under continual psychiatric care and mental health treatment for more than ten years. The way he asked the hospital questions also had me confirming that Chris had been admitted each time because of suicide attempts, suicidal ideation, or threats of harm to himself or others. Technically, I was supposed to leave the courtroom after testifying, but at my lawyer's request, the judge ruled I could stay to hear the remaining testimony.

After I sat down on my bench with Will, the prosecutor called the MHMRA psychologist to testify. He rose from the seat behind us and walked to the witness stand to testify as the state's second witness. The prosecutor asked him to explain the process followed in conducting Chris's sanity evaluations and how the conclusion that he was sane at the time of the stabbing of his father had been reached. There were three sanity evaluations submitted to the court that had been conducted by different MHMRA psychologists. The evaluations were completed on September 30, 2009, April 22, 2010, and July 21, 2011—all after Chris was deemed competent to stand trial and his discharge from Vernon State Hospital in August 2009. All three reports stated the opinion that Chris was sane on June 29, 2005. However, despite their professional opinions about Chris's sanity, the psychologists had also placed qualifying statements in the reports acknowledging the severity of Chris's mental illness, concluding:

- "Continued psychiatric treatment for his schizoaffective disorder, including psychotropic medication, will be important to maintain Mr. Malone's emotional and behavioral stability." *September 30, 2009*

- "Ongoing psychiatric care for Mr. Malone's schizoaffective disorder will be critical in maintaining his emotional and behavioral stability. Treatment should include but not necessarily be limited to the use of psychoactive medication and participation in cognitive behavioral therapy." *April 22, 2010*

- "Based on clinical interview, review of available records and observation, it is the opinion of this examiner that Mr. Malone likely exhibited the mental illness of psychotic disorder not otherwise specified (NOS) at the time of the alleged offense." *July 21, 2011*

When Chris's attorney questioned the MHMRA psychologist, he primarily asked for more detail about the steps that had been taken in conducting the sanity evaluations. His questions took the form of confirming what the examining psychologists had *not* done. The attorney asked if MHMRA had subpoenaed Chris's records from the thirteen psychiatric outpatient and inpatient hospital admissions where he had received treatment during the ten years prior to Rob's death. He asked if any of Chris's family members, including myself, had been interviewed about Chris's psychiatric history. The witness answered no to those questions. With the exception of records from Chris's hospitalization at Rusk State Hospital in 2002, the examining psychologists for MHMRA had solely relied on the forensic records of Chris's treatment and behavior since his incarceration and hospitalization following Rob's stabbing, along with the fifty-minute interviews each psychologist held with Chris during the sanity evaluations.

As I listened to this testimony, I compared what the psychologist was saying on the stand with the ambivalence of the three reports' concluding statements. Yes, they all agreed that Chris should be considered to have been legally sane on or about the time of his alleged offense, and, yes, Chris was clearly mentally ill. It seemed that a lot of weight was given to statements made by Chris in interviews conducted four, five, and six years after Rob's death. In 2009 the report said that Chris stated to the psychologist, "I snapped . . . The stabbing was an impulse. I never had done anything like that before." The report of the 2010 interview documented Chris's statement to the psychologist as "I guess I knew at the time it was wrong." Finally in 2011 Chris told the psychologist, "I was aware that murder was wrong. I just lost control." As an intimate witness to this entire event from hell, I could see Chris's calm explanations were absolutely off target! He was in a hostile state at 10:00 a.m. that day because the telepaths (Rob and I) were putting thoughts into his head, taking thoughts out of his head, laughing at him, and saying derogatory things behind his back. And he was still feeling and thinking the same way at 12:30 p.m. when Rob returned home from teaching. Of course Chris knew murder was wrong! We'd taught him that. It was a core belief of each person in our family. I felt very confused and reflected on my own testimony about that day. Who would the judge believe, Chris's mother or the MHMRA psychologists?

Of course Chris knew murder was wrong! We'd taught him that. It was a core belief of each person in our family.

As I listened to his testimony, I thought the MHMRA psychologist on the stand surely saw the ambiguity in these three reports just as I did. I did not know what legal and medical factors and limitations could or could not be considered when making a determination of sanity during an event that happened almost seven years before. Neither attorney asked any questions on that particular topic. But the state's witness did not appear to take any pleasure in reporting the psychologists' opinions about Chris's sanity on June 29, 2005.

The defense opened its part of the trial by calling the independent psychiatrist to testify. Since I had not seen him prior to this moment, I quickly felt relieved when I saw him walk into the courtroom. He must have been waiting in the hallway outside the courtroom. Why had I continued to worry? I knew God was in charge this day of all days.

His testimony was very interesting to me. While I had read an early draft of the report and knew many documents had been subpoenaed, I had seen none of the supporting documents. The final report that was submitted to the court was twenty-nine pages long. The psychiatrist had reviewed and deciphered approximately two thousand pages of medical records, recommitment examinations and orders for competency determination, and reports made by the Dangerousness Review Board. He also had examined law enforcement and DA records, including the indictment, supporting documents for Chris's application for Social Security Disability, and the Doctor's Mental Status Examination for Guardianship completed by Chris's psychiatrist during his last hospitalization before Rob died. Additionally, he had reviewed news accounts of Rob's stabbing and read statements from Rob and Will describing Chris's state of mind a few months before June 29, 2005. Finally he had met with Chris and me individually and conducted interviews that lasted almost three hours each. I had given him excerpts of a journal Chris wrote while at Vernon. Chris had mailed the journal to me for safekeeping just before he was transferred to Harris County jail for the last time, in August 2009. He had just been found competent to stand trial, and he and I both knew he was in the best mental state he had been in for a long time. I thought he was as competent as he could be under the circumstances. He gave me permission to read the journal and then share it with his attorney if I thought it would be helpful in the case. Chris was terrified of the possibility of being sent to prison, and his delusions of being tortured were always in the front of his mind.

Much of the psychiatrist's testimony centered on the thoroughly documented reports of the lengthiness of Chris's mental illness, the multiple serious instances of self-harm, and the consistency in his reported symptoms throughout his years of treatment. He focused on the two hospitalizations in January and April 2005, just weeks before Rob's death. He testified that the hospital records from both 2005 hospitalizations documented the opinion of the attending psychiatrists that stimulant medications such as Adderall exacerbate psychosis and therefore were contraindicated in Chris's case. Consequently, Adderall had been removed from Chris's medication regimen while in the hospital and was not prescribed as one of his medications at the time of discharge. Another significant point of the testimony regarding Adderall concerned the postdated prescription for Adderall that I had found in Rob's wallet after he died. It was written at Chris's June 23 appointment but was dated "7/5/05," seven days after Rob's death. Chris's regular psychiatrist not only had disagreed with the medication regimen ordered by the hospital psychiatrists but also had violated rules governing prescriptions for controlled substances.

In his testimony the independent psychiatrist shed some light on why I had been unable to answer certain of the prosecutor's questions in my earlier testimony. The psychiatrist testified that Chris had told him that he had "yelled at his father to turn onto his back to stop the bleeding, saying, 'On your back, disciple!' " This might have been the statement the prosecutor was questioning me about earlier. I don't remember hearing Chris say this or even being aware that he was in the kitchen when I was trying to call 911. Maybe he said it after I ran outside to look for someone to help me dial 911. Did he walk back into the kitchen while I was not present and issue this command to his dad? I only know that Rob was alone and leaning against the kitchen counter when I came back inside.

It was unexpected but not surprising that the prosecutor found a sticky point for cross-examination concerning Chris's current state of competency. In his written report and testimony, the psychiatrist had analyzed all the times while Chris was at Vernon State Hospital that he had needed special medication and restraint due to florid psychotic symptoms. During Chris's first twenty-one-month stay, this had occurred nineteen times. In addition, Chris had needed extra medication to calm the psychotic symptoms following his competency evaluations. He also noted that Chris was able to maintain a calm, cooperative demeanor for a little more than an hour in his psych interview before gradually becoming more and more guarded, suspicious of the doctor's motives, and ultimately too agitated to continue the interview. The doctor had terminated his three-hour interview with Chris to prevent further deterioration in Chris's mental status and to preserve his safety. His conclusion, based on the Vernon record and his experience with Chris during the interview, was that, in general, Chris was able to hold it together for about an hour in a one-on-one interpersonal situation before the internal voices, delusions, and paranoia began to interfere with his clarity of thought and ability to maintain composure, or competency in legal terms.

> Judge Wallace grabbed his gavel, declared, "Not guilty by reason of insanity," pounded the gavel on its base, stood up, and left the courtroom without another word.

While listening to the lengthy discussion among the lawyers, testifying psychiatrist, and the judge, I felt like Competency was standing in the middle of the court room and screaming that it was Chris's grandiose nemesis. The psychiatrist stated that competency could be a changing state in a person who is seriously mentally ill. He also said that Chris was competent during the first part of the interview, and then he basically became not competent because of a flare-up of psychotic symptoms. What the judge and prosecutor seemed to focus on was their concern for the legal validity of the trial itself if this expert witness was saying that the defendant was not competent. All of this made sense to me, common sense. There is the legal term "competent to stand trial," meaning understanding your legal situation and being able to work with your attorney for your defense. Secondly, there is the psychological term "competent," meaning qualified or capable of performing a certain life duty or activity. During this trial Chris was competent according to both definitions. He had been sitting quietly beside his attorney, paying perfect attention to all the testimony, and giving no indication of mental disturbances in his behavior, body language, or facial expression. Finally the testimony about Chris's pattern of intermittent competency for short durations of time was allowed by the judge. The doctor then concluded his testimony, ensuring that the trial would last not much longer than one hour.

After the psychiatrist left the witness stand, the judge asked first the defense attorney and then the prosecutor if they had anything else to put before the court. They each stood and told the judge, "No, Your Honor."

Immediately Judge Wallace grabbed his gavel, declared, "Not guilty by reason of insanity," pounded the gavel on its base, stood up, and left the courtroom without another word. I was not the only person dumbfounded by this sudden conclusion to the trial. Will and I looked at each other, and one of us asked, "What did he say?"

We figured out the judge's ruling quickly enough, and all I wanted to know then was what would happen to Chris next. A bailiff escorted him back to the holding cell, and his lawyer and the psychiatrist walked us out to the hallway. The MHMRA psychologist came up to me to shake my hand and said he was so sorry for my loss and all the heartache we had been through as a family. He wished the best for Chris and hoped he would get all the treatment he so badly needed. He wished me well, said he was happy for me, and hoped that the outcome of the trial would allow me to go on with peace in my life. I appreciated this stranger's kind words and momentarily remembered that no such expression of sympathy or well wishes had come from Chris's own psychiatrist, who had sat in his office with Rob and Chris six days before his patient experienced the episode of psychotic rage that had resulted in Rob's death. The MHMRA psychologist then left me with my family and Chris's legal team for hugs, smiles, and tears of joy and relief all around.

A Note About the Independent Psychiatrist

When Chris's defense attorney received his copy of the first MHMRA sanity evaluation in 2009, which concluded that Chris was sane at the time he had killed his father, the attorney immediately petitioned the judge to authorize an outside, independent professional to conduct a separate sanity evaluation of Chris. The judge granted the motion at the following month's hearing.

The defense attorney contacted a psychiatrist who was on staff at Baylor College of Medicine as a clinical associate professor in the Menninger Department of Psychiatry and Behavioral Sciences. He held a joint appointment on the faculty of the University of Texas Medical School at Houston as a clinical assistant professor in the Department of Psychiatry and Behavioral Sciences. His evaluation and compilation of Chris's long, tumultuous history of mental illness stunned me with its comprehensiveness and straightforwardness. When I first read the draft of his report many months before the trial, I felt as if I were seeing my life as a huge, ugly splat on the floor that the whole world was now privy to. It brought back years of traumatizing experiences as if they had happened just yesterday. But it was also clear that he felt tremendous compassion and respect for us in how we had persevered in seeking treatment for Chris. The manner in which he conducted Chris's evaluation and its thoroughness must stand as a model to the entire mental health profession. His participation in Chris's case was a great gift from God.

I felt as if I were seeing my life as a huge, ugly splat on the floor that the whole word was now privy to.

Part Five

WHAT I LEARNED THAT MIGHT HELP YOU

20

About Delusions and Voices

One of the biggest barriers to eliminating the stigma of mental illness is the inability of a mentally healthy person to think like a mentally ill, psychotic person. Experiencing what a thought disorder like schizophrenia or schizoaffective disorder really feels like inside your own mind is rarely physically possible unless you experience psychosis induced by drugs or certain other neurological diseases or you endure a mental health professional's training exercise wearing a schizophrenia simulator. If you want to try to understand the intense mental confusion created by psychotic symptoms, you can only imagine the sounds, sensations, feelings, and rapid, disjointed thoughts that a person who is mentally ill is experiencing. At the time these things are happening, the voices, thoughts, and feelings are all real for the ill person. They do not just seem real; *they are real.* They are not part of the person's imagination, like it was for me when I tried to understand what was happening in Chris's mind or when I try to explain delusions and voices to someone else. I am sure that Chris did not imagine that the children next door were saying bad things about him; he heard the children say the words in his head. The command "Kill yourself on TV" was the actual sound of a voice speaking to him from the television. The delusions that he was being persecuted by telepaths everywhere, being stalked by the FBI in the woods in New Mexico, and threatened by the cable guy who was planting listening devices in our cable boxes were all facts to Chris.

Can you imagine yourself suddenly believing for a fact that these unjust, unfair, illegal, and mean things were happening to you, causing you to feel fully exposed, unprotected, and in danger? What if you were surrounded by people who were

- calling you names when you were minding your own business?
- ridiculing you on and on when you were trying to avoid and ignore them?
- committing secretive acts and spying on you when you just wanted to live a normal, private life?
- telling you to do harmful things to yourself or someone you love?
- telling you not to trust someone who you knew loved you?

Psychosis is the ultimate bully. Going inside your own house and into your own bedroom cannot shut the bully out. He is with you 24/7 and speaks up whenever he wants to. In a moment of frustration, I may casually say, "I'm losing my mind," because I can't find my car keys. My forgetting doesn't mean I am losing my mind, but Chris's psychotic symptoms meant he was losing his mind.

Psychosis is the ultimate bully. Going inside your own house and into your own bedroom cannot shut the bully out. He is with you 24/7 and speaks up whenever he wants.

Chris's brain simply did not work like it was supposed to. The chemical components and neurons of his brain delivered wrong messages to his thinking brain, his sensing brain, and his emotional brain. The parts of his brain that controlled physical movement and involuntary movement (breathing, heart rate, digestion, balance) worked normally. That is why mental illness is often considered an invisible disease. It does not show on the outside unless the individual is severely mentally ill; then there is likely something in the person's manner or facial expression that is noticeable. When you live with it daily, side by side with someone you love, you know mental illness is real. It is not simply bad behavior or manners, manipulation, poor or weak character, or poor parenting.

We call this disease "mental illness," which seems like vague terminology to me. The general public does not have a concept of what is really wrong with a person who is mentally ill as we do when we hear someone has heart disease or cancer. Where is Chris's "mental"? I don't have a "mental," and neither do you or Chris. It is more accurate to say that Chris has a brain illness, and like heart disease and cancer, it can be at least mildly debilitating and at worst deadly.

We were totally unable to prevent, contain, or stop the powerful force of the psychotic rage that was fueled by his mental illness.

On the afternoon of June 29, 2005, I did not know that Chris had been overhearing Rob and me as he sat quietly in the living room. I thought he was upstairs in his bedroom and the conversation between Rob and me was private. I was wrong. Chris was having his own conversation in his head; the vicious, laughing voices were screaming belittling comments. The voices were on a rampage, and his paranoia was racing at full speed. While our reality at the moment was excitement and the expectation of a new job for Rob, Chris's reality was a threat and danger from us. We were totally unable to prevent, contain, or stop the powerful force of the psychotic rage that was fueled by his mental illness.

Over time as I learned more about Chris's illness, I gradually understood that mental illness is not only difficult to diagnose and treat, but the roller-coaster ride is scariest for my son. Chris was in a psychotic state when he attacked us on June 29. Clearly, that day was my worst experience with my mentally ill son. Nothing in his mind was working like yours or mine that day. He was living in a totally different reality.

Several years after Rob's death, Chris was able to tell me a little of what was happening in his head that day. He said the voices were screaming in his head. He kept telling them in his mind, "Shut up; shut up!" He was thinking that "all the sordid little details of my life were being broadcast all around." He felt huge anger and paranoia and became enraged as he listened to us "laugh at and make fun of" him. We were an overwhelming threat to him with our powers as telepaths. All his anger exploded when I asked him, "Did you kick the dog?" Later, when Steve and I visited him at the jail the evening before Rob's funeral, Chris told me his dad was his best friend. The next day the voices rebuked him for calling Rob "my best friend" instead of "my father."

Before Rob's death when we would talk calmly about his symptoms, Chris had described the voices to me as a rushing wind popping or clapping in his inner ear, laughter, or low whispers. The words and phrases he consistently heard were "Fag," "You devil!" "Don't talk to her!" "You bet," and "Caught." These words and short phrases were said with a mocking tone of voice and ridiculed him with derisive laughter. He said that when he was hospitalized, he heard voices that told him, "Don't talk about it. Don't say a word to the doctors," and so he did not. How many times did I read in his medical records these comments of hospital staff and psychiatrists: "Denies suicidal ideation," "Denies hearing voices," "States he feels okay; is not depressed." There he was in a psychiatric hospital, often by court order, and Chris was saying, "Everything is peachy!"

Before I started to write this book, I spoke to Chris on the phone and told him what I was planning to do. In our next phone conversation one week later, he said immediately after getting off the phone with me the previous week a voice told him to "totally cut ties with her." The next day a voice threatened "to torture him and cut him in two" if he helped me write this book. The result of hearing these voices caused Chris again to distrust me and my motives.

He still thought of me as a telepath and, therefore, I was a danger to him. He did not understand that it was the voice that made the overt threat "to torture him."

> With the benefit of God's wisdom, I learned that confronting, convincing, insisting, even strongly suggesting or persuading were ill-advised where Chris was concerned.

Apparently, telling Chris to cut ties with me was a fairly frequent demand of the voices. With the benefit of God's wisdom, I learned that confronting, convincing, insisting, even strongly suggesting or persuading were ill-advised where Chris was concerned. For the most part, he and I could communicate fairly well without animosity during the time he was incarcerated and hospitalized following Rob's death. I did not want to cause him any distress; he'd had enough of that already on a daily basis. I mostly tried to listen and encourage, or we just chatted about simple things.

Chris told me that at times the voices would come in waves. He described those experiences as psychic attacks or psychic hurricanes. They would come on a regular schedule it seems, usually on Monday evenings. His psychiatrist adjusted his antipsychotic medication many times, either by increasing the dosage, giving it earlier in the afternoon, or changing or deleting part of his medication regimen. When I listened to his description of the voices coming in furious waves, I was reminded of how migraine headaches would come on me when I was younger. Today, Chris does for his psychotic attacks what I did for my migraines years ago: medication, darkness, quiet, and no human interaction. After my migraine would subside following several hours of rest, I always felt drained physically, mentally, and emotionally, and somewhat dizzy and groggy when I finally left my bedroom and rejoined the world. Chris's psychotic attacks affect him in a similar way.

Chris continued to experience the same delusions of telepathy, persecution, and paranoia throughout his periods of incarceration and hospitalization after

Rob's death. Following his trial and the determination that he was not guilty by reason of insanity, he was transferred by court order to North Texas State Hospital for long-term treatment. His symptoms of psychosis have lessened in frequency and intensity since the trial in November 2011. But he still has breakthrough psychotic symptoms that medication and treatment have not eradicated.

Schizoaffective disorder is not a curable illness, but it can be treated. Unfortunately, the science of treatment at times is more akin to the art of treatment. Minimizing the stressfulness of daily life, maintaining compliance with medication, gaining insight into the illness, and relearning how to build trusting relationships are the treatment goals.

His core belief system is bounded by paranoia and distrust. My core belief system is bounded by God's love and mercy.

Chris's inner voices and delusions have been his reality for a very long time, thirteen years. How long will it take for him to recover to a state of mind in which he can return to a reality similar to the one the Malone family experienced before mental illness came into our lives?

This question does not have an answer because Chris's inner voices and delusions are linked so closely. The voices increase the intensity and truthfulness of his delusional thoughts and feelings, while the delusional thoughts and feelings give power and validity to the voices. Together they form the foundation of his belief system and underlie his perception of reality. His core belief system is bounded by paranoia and distrust. My core belief system is bounded by God's love and mercy.

During several recent phone conversations with Chris, I asked him to share with me some details of the voices and delusions he experiences that I could include in this book. He knows that I think what he "hears" is part of the mental illness symptoms. His view is different. He thinks they are real and often refers to them either as demons or God, who he thinks is punishing him.

About Delusions and Voices

With reluctance Chris agreed to tell me about the voices and delusions. He is now hospitalized in an intermediate security program at the Wichita Falls Campus of North Texas State Hospital. This is a closely supervised program where he resides, participates in life-adjustment classes, and receives medication and treatment. He will remain under the supervision of Harris County District Court 263 either until he is "cured" or the maximum period of the sentence of the crime for which he originally was indicted is reached. The charge was felony murder, and it has a maximum sentence of life imprisonment.

Chris is much more stable now than he was in 2005, but he continues to experience auditory hallucinations and paranoid delusions. The following is Chris's description of the voices and delusions as he has experienced them for the past thirteen years since the psychotic symptoms first appeared as whispers in the fall of 2000:

> Not all the voices are literal at the beginning. They start out as a feeling, and I can sense a kind of mood swing coming on. Then the voices start up. I think they want to wear me down, take away my hope, and make me feel miserable. Over time the voices have grown more evil and constant. The day after I was baptized, February 5, 2001, a voice said, "Everything is meaningless." When I used to listen to my radio in my bedroom at home, the voices I heard were often talking about me. I would hear statements over the radio that said my exact thought, so I knew the radio was telepathic and could plant thoughts in my mind. That still happens now in the hospital. It also meant the whole world could hear my thoughts because the radio was broadcasting them all over.
>
> Sometimes the voices say one or two words or phrases. Other times they tell me specifically to do or not do something. When I broke my neck in the hospital, I heard a voice that

came from the TV and told me, "Kill yourself on TV." That's when I ran and jumped on top of the television set and dived off headfirst. Sometimes I now hear a voice saying, "At least we're walking." I think the voice is referring to the time I broke my neck. One of the first voices I heard after the whispers started said, "You're caught," meaning I'm in trouble or I'm guilty. Other voices call me "faggot" or "slave." Another says sarcastically, "You bet," as if nothing I ever think or say is true and no one will ever believe me. Some days I hear these voices in streams for a long period of time. They won't stop. I can't make them stop.

Here at the hospital I continually hear the staff and other patients calling me names and laughing at me. They are the voices of doom and my constant critics, making me feel like I am a lower caste than they are. I think the voices want to prevent any forward momentum in my life. They are discouraging. They tell me to "quit your job"; "don't read that book—it's a sin to read,"—two of the things I like and can do here at the hospital. Since I have been working here at the hospital, I hear a "money voice." It is like an entity in my head that criticizes and rebukes me for costing everyone so much money. It was talking in my head when I was on the phone with Mom and she was telling me about the book. The words I hear are external sounds inside my head. I infer their meaning based on the sense of fear and paranoia that I am feeling when I hear the voice. When the staff, doctors, or patients ask me questions, the voices become louder, more demanding, and derogatory. [Recall my question to Chris—"Did you kick the dog?"—that triggered his rage on June 29, 2005.]

The voices were bad at the time of Dad's death. I was stark-raving mad with superstitions and magical thinking, and they got worse after Dad died. My experience in the solitary cell proved that they wanted to hurt me. When I was in the solitary cell right after my arrest, all kinds of weird stuff happened. I could hear things coming from a TV or radio that would sound comedic and hilarious; then what I was hearing would switch and sound paranoid and hostile. I thought the TV was trying to eat me. It was projecting my mind to the real world and projecting the real world's mind to me. The voices went up and down in volume. I had a sensation like I was witnessing a drive-by drug deal. I saw a small dancing teddy bear that reminded me of a Smurf. He comforted me and kept me company for a while. It was all just weird, stressful, odd, and scary. I had a lot of other visual and auditory hallucinations that I don't want to talk about. I did not take any medication during this four-month period of time in jail.

Lately I've heard some positive voices; they sound like encouraging statements. A voice will say, "Everything's okay" or "You're a miracle." I try to take these voices at face value and believe they want to make me feel good about myself, but I'm not sure if this is true. I don't think the voices are honest with me. I think they use the positive statements to bait me, to pull me in.

The voices want me to fail. They put me on a guilt trip. They tell me that I am supposed to fight, but I don't want to. They threaten, scold, mock, and belittle me. Not too long ago I started to talk openly to the psychologist, and then the voices got worse. By worse, I mean they constantly said things rather than coming in waves at different times of the day. The comments are all negative. I stopped going to my therapy appointment because the voices reprimanded me for revealing too much. To sum up, I feel like if I don't jump through their hoops, I will get hurt.

— Chris

My Depiction of the Voices

I am immensely grateful that Chris has allowed me to include his description of the voices. I feel inadequate to explain what is going on inside my own mind at times, much less tell what is happening inside another person's mind. As humans, our minds tell us who we are. The mind defines us as unique individuals and is the only truly, private place we have in life. Despite the automatic revelations of our body language, facial expressions, and tone of voice, we can hide our most private thoughts from others. Only if we trust and choose to share these thoughts are they known to any other person. Chris has trusted me with some of the secrets of his voices, and I see this as a tremendous step forward in his healing and a great blessing from God.

21

God and My Coping Strategies

When I look back over this period of my life stretching from Chris's teenage years to now, my retirement years, I can pick out coping strategies I have used. I see them in the ways I faced our problems, fears, and confusion. I absolutely know that I did not see this clearly at the time we were speeding along the roller-coaster tracks of Chris's mental illness. But I believe God endows human beings with an intellect and a strong connection to our surroundings that enable us to develop coping strategies on the run when we find ourselves in a crisis situation.

Professional Helpers and New Learning

When Chris was a thirteen-year-old marijuana user, his behavior reached its first troubling peak, and we turned to trusted professionals—a licensed counselor and our family doctor. When his acting-out escalated into a fourteen-year-old manic runaway episode, we turned to a specialist, a child and adolescent psychiatrist. After his first hospitalization at age fifteen, we connected with an experienced counselor who became Chris's long-term therapist and our most trusted consultant. It was so clear to Rob and me, especially after those first three major events, that we had to have professional help for both ourselves and our son.

Later when Chris was twenty years old and he began hearing whispers, I had a deep gut feeling that something awful was moving in on Chris. In his next appointment with the psychiatrist, following his admission to me about the whispers, Chris was given a prescription for a new drug that I'd not heard of before. When I turned in the prescription at the drugstore, I asked the pharmacist what it was used for. When he returned ten minutes later with the filled prescription, he also handed me a sticky note on which he had written "schizophrenia." The medication was Abilify. Had God just tipped me off that Rob and I should gird ourselves for a rocky road ahead? Chris has taken Ability off and on for thirteen years since that first prescription was filled, alternating with other antipsychotic medications, to help with his psychotic symptoms.

The important thing about turning to professionals for help with an acting-out adolescent was that we had to be willing to learn many new things—different ways of parenting, looking openly at the strengths and weaknesses of our marriage relationship, and facing problems with a different attitude, one of perseverance and patience. We learned big new ideas and small new ideas. They all turned out to be important. Rob was the "thinker parent," and he needed to learn how to become more of a "feeling parent." I was the "feeling parent," and I needed to learn how to become more of a "thinker parent." This did not mean Rob and I were poor parents, but it did mean that we needed new approaches in dealing with new behaviors. Rob became a better listener and less authoritarian in nature over time. I became more focused and better able to enforce the house rules consistently. Most importantly, we learned to communicate openly with each other about our differences of perception, our feelings, and our thoughts on what was the best thing to do. We learned to ask questions of any professional who was helping our son. Their answers strengthened our understanding and instincts in responding to difficult situations with Chris. My learning curve about mental illness is still going up sharply.

The Value of Teamwork

Not every family can pull as a team in facing such a serious illness. Not every parent has a partner to share the burden, not only of the responsibilities, but also of the heartache, fear, and confusion that are so prevalent in major illnesses and family disruption. This fact hit me squarely between the eyes after Rob died. I felt incapable of completing the simplest chores and making everyday decisions. This may sound petty and insignificant, but it didn't feel that way at the time. Rob had always carried out the garbage, fed the pets, locked up the house at night, and made the morning coffee. After he died, it seemed that I either resented having to do those things myself (making coffee and feeding pets), took forever to accomplish the chore (taking out the garbage), or felt incompetent to do it securely and without forgetting (locking up at night). I know that period was part of my grieving process, and I eventually got past it. It took time for me to begin to trust my abilities to make it alone, but I still missed Rob doing those things for me.

If you do not have a team, try to get one.

If you do not have a team, try to get one. Start with the professionals you have contacted, and use them until you get a simple plan together. Unfortunately, the first inclination we had was to keep all of Chris's troubles to ourselves. Shame and guilt automatically joined us on our mental illness journey. The first people Rob and I told about Chris's illness were our parents. They tried to understand and support us, but it was hard at times because this was all new to them too. Next our immediate supervisors at work were brought into the loop. Chris had too many close calls medically, and Rob and I had to deal with emergencies, doctors' appointments, and hospital time. We were also open in talking to Will about his brother's problems. I have never thought keeping secrets benefited important personal relationships, and Will had a right to know what was happening in his family even though he was away at college.

Another valuable group of team members for us were the two support groups we attended as a family. There is anonymity in most support groups. NAMI and PDAP were safe places to air out our anger, whether it was something specific about Chris's doctor or school or something general regarding society, drugs, or God's purpose in all our pain and worry. We most certainly learned coping skills from other parents, and they learned from us. Mental illness is such a leveler of the field because not knowing personal information about others in the group removes any sense of competitiveness that parents often experience when a group starts talking about their kids' behavior. I didn't know which kids were in gifted-and-talented classes or were great athletes, nor did I know where or if parents worked or what neighborhoods they lived in. At first I did not want to ask strangers for help. It was hard enough to tell people who loved and respected me about what was happening in our family. But with Chris's symptoms intensifying, and treatment and medication not helping as much as we hoped, the support groups provided us with encouragement and a nonjudgmental peer group. The groups became valuable networks for us, and we learned about new approaches and ideas that had worked for others.

My family—Will, Steve, and Patty—have always been invaluable teammates and great supporters, especially immediately after Rob's death. Steve and Patty continually gave wise counsel and remained grounded when I cried out for answers that were not there. Steve especially was a support in driving me to see Chris at the jail and at the hospital in Vernon. Just having him behind the wheel and standing by my side in case I crumbled was my greatest coping strategy during those extremely stressful trips. From the beginning, Will helped me make financial, legal, and medical decisions.

When Will drove with me to see Chris in Vernon, he sat with me through one of the most painful sessions I'd ever had with a counselor. That's when I learned the ugly details of what had happened to Chris during his first four months in Harris County jail.

Will knows all my financial secrets, including my occasional poor spending choices and great need for a trusted adviser. Since Will lived in another city when his dad was killed and he had a family and job, he could not drop everything and come to my rescue when I felt like having a pity party. It hurt him that he could not be with me at those times. I know he is thankful for my other teammates who gave me support, especially since he also suffered a great loss and had his own grief and sense of unreality to face.

My team also included four close girlfriends I'd shared our troubles with years before when Chris was hospitalized several times in one year. Interestingly, I worked with all of them, but we became much more than coworkers over the years. After Rob's death they were especially supportive to me. They spent time with me going to Chris's hearings, treated me to lunch and Friday night dinners, sent me notes of encouragement, invited me over for special holidays, prayed with and for me, and much more. I could not have gotten along without my team. We have cried and been sad together and have laughed and had fun together. They were God's earliest angels on my saddest day, June 29, 2005, and they are still doing His good works.

Reality, Instincts, and Patterns

When it came right down to responding to a crisis with Chris, Rob and I did not have our team waiting around us. In fact, we were often either exhausted and lounging in our pj's, intensely committed to our task of the moment, or finally enjoying a few minutes to relax and have fun. The team helped train, prepare, and encourage us, and afterward they helped us deal with the blowback.

What helped us handle an emergency or emotional blowup or dangerous situation were our internal resources. We learned quickly to face the reality at hand. Could we handle this on our own, or did we need help? We became very good at quickly assessing the seriousness of what was happening with Chris. For example, when Chris overdosed on LSD at school, I called the psychiatrist. By the time the school notified us, it had been a few hours since Chris had ingested the drug. I asked his doctor if we should take him to the emergency room. The doctor told us to take him home and let him sleep it off since it appeared he had already made it through the worst part of ingesting the drug. He told us to stay with Chris and go immediately to the ER if he later had a bad reaction. Having this as a "professional" guideline, we were often able to use our own judgment about making an ER run versus monitoring him at home and providing common-sense treatments. Sometimes Rob was the best judge because he figured out that Chris was extremely drunk rather than drugged. A minor distinction, but Rob had seen drunks before and knew better how to gauge Chris's condition.

Feeling frozen with fear or scared to death is not a good place to be in the middle of an emergency.

We learned that quickly looking at the reality of the situation pushed us into a problem-solving mind-set and helped prevent our becoming overwhelmed with emotion. Feeling frozen with fear or scared to death is not a good place to be in the middle of an emergency. This coping strategy came into play for me when Chris and Rob were standing above me and fighting. I knew I had to get out of their way; I had to move from underneath them. Greater harm truly was imminent, but I just didn't know exactly what was coming. When Chris tried to jump out of the car on the way to the medical center, we knew we had to calm him down. We could not drive twenty-five miles at freeway speed and expect to arrive with a living son if he kept trying to get away from us. Rob's calming voice was truly a life-saving gift that day. On another occasion we let the US marshals take Chris for an emergency psychiatric evaluation at the medical center. We had learned that driving with him a long distance in traffic when he was suicidal or psychotic was too dangerous for us to attempt on our own. I did not like handing over my son to be handcuffed by law enforcement officers just because he was in need of medical attention. That was a harsh reality to face.

The most difficult reality I faced was when it became clear to me that I was not in charge of curing Chris of his horrible mental illness and psychotic symptoms. The problem was so much bigger than I, as his parent, could handle. I clearly remember this moment of insight and my willingness to recognize I was powerless over his mental illness. My making Chris well had been a mirage. In the big scheme of things, that is the best reality I could have faced and accepted. Powerlessness does not equate with helplessness. Help was available, not perfect help, but enough for me to maintain hope and to keep putting one foot in front of the other. God still is in charge, and my faith has only been strengthened as He has continued to guide and comfort me in this life. His promise is to walk with me through troubled times, not prevent them from coming into my life.

When I paid close attention, I often intuitively sensed that something did not feel right about Chris's explanations and behaviors. Another strategy that was a close ally of following my instincts was remaining calm and not reacting in anger or in an accusatory manner. I know this led Chris to be more forthcoming with us. This is not a new parenting strategy, but the stakes were always high because of the severity of his mental illness and his skewed psychotic reality. There is no doubt that most parents can sense when a child is up to mischief. Remaining calm when I confronted Chris kept the situation safer. This was probably one of the most difficult coping strategies for me, because I always felt so stressed with life. I described how hypervigilant Rob and I became, especially when Chris's suicidal attempts seemed to supersede almost everything we thought and did. It was easy to overreact, especially to relatively minor incidents.

Learning to respond calmly and patiently also helped me after Rob died. When he died, I lost my best friend, my partner in life, and my costrategist. Rob was an analytical thinker, and I was a close observer of human behavior.

We definitely were stronger as a team of two than I was on my own without him. After he died, I set careful boundaries for my conversations with Chris. I had two reasons. One was that Chris still expressed so much suicidal ideation and hostile rage that I was afraid of what he might do if somehow I set him off as I did when I asked if he had kicked the dog. This was especially true during the first four years when Chris was either in jail or in the hospital.

The second reason I was careful in communicating with him was that his criminal case was still hanging over us. My instincts told me to stay clear of what I thought, felt, knew, or had said to a lawyer or prosecutor or what they had said to me. I'm not sure why I decided to follow my instincts in this particular matter unless it was God's guidance, but I had set these boundaries from the very beginning, after Chris was arrested. I stayed with open-ended questions when we spoke on the phone. If he said, "I don't want to talk about it" or came back with a tense, agitated response, I just said okay and changed the subject. Mostly I encouraged him to do the things he could to manage his own life. He complained of not trusting his treatment team and would not tell them how many problems he was experiencing, either with his psychotic symptoms or the side effects of his medication. I suggested that he write down what he wanted to tell the treatment team before his meetings. That way he could be sure to describe what he was experiencing in the way he wanted to say it. He often took my suggestions that were given in this way. I suppose I was trying to teach him some coping strategies, something we both needed.

In addition to learning to keep a calm attitude, I enhanced my effectiveness by seeing patterns in Chris's behavior. When he spent a morning looking morose, staring out the window, and not talking and then started the afternoon hostile, angry, loud, and demanding, I knew he had had a mood swing. To me, angry, hostile mood swings were scarier than depressed mood swings. Granted, Chris attempted suicide in a depressed state of mind and nearly succeeded with the Zyprexa overdose. But whenever he had a manic mood swing, especially one with psychotic features, he became unpredictable, and my sense of potential danger grew. After the delusions became fixed in his mind as his reality, Chris was frequently afraid of being tortured by the government or being taken over by the telepaths. That was a good time to keep it low key in the house. No visitors. No blaring television. As low a stress level as possible. I am sure many outbursts were avoided when we were able to anticipate what was distressing Chris and head it off in that way. My telling Chris to go to his room when he was screaming about being my god or was threatening "I may have to kill you" served the purpose of putting him in a safe, quiet place. The next time he came downstairs, usually two hours later, he would often be calm and able to interact with us safely. I also learned to trust that when he went out the front door in anger, he was going to take a long walk. I know he walked miles and miles before coming back home in a calmer state of mind. That became a frequent pattern, one of Chris's most-used, safe coping strategies.

I am sure many outbursts were avoided when we were able to anticipate what was distressing Chris and head it off in that way.

Caring for Yourself

Because Chris's mental illness seemed to consume us, Rob and I were not very good about caring for ourselves. Rob and I both fell on the introvert side of the personality spectrum but not totally. We were successful at jobs that required leadership and problem-solving abilities. We both worked in people-based organizations and daily were involved with others through our work. I recognized a hidden coping strategy as I have gone about writing this story, along with reviewing and revising it many times. I noticed all the instances where I mentioned that a calm attitude or soft voice from someone else in the midst of our tumult was helpful to me. This is one way I was able to center myself in the midst of chaos. When we consciously turned down the noise and stress levels in our household for Chris's sake, Rob and I also benefited.

We also had our own ways of giving a little time to ourselves. I am an avid reader, and even if I had time for only a few pages of my current mystery novel, I managed to keep that in my schedule on most days. We had a concrete bench in the front yard that was partially hidden by large azalea bushes, and one of my favorite moments was to have a cup of coffee alone on that bench. I also loved to work in my flower beds, but there was rarely time for that. While having my coffee on the bench, I might pull a weed or two.

Rob had his own quiet ways of self-care too. He loved music and would pick up his guitar or sit down at the piano or grab a harmonica and make a few sounds whenever he could. His workbench in the garage was a special place for Rob. He would spend time arranging and sorting tools. He didn't have time to launch into any major projects, but he loved spending time alone with his tools. Will and some friends of mine would rather slam a tennis ball or go for a run or lift a few weights as a way of taking care of themselves. Just a few moments here and there in an activity that was personally refreshing helped prepare us for the next crisis.

My being kind to my spouse and his being kind to me were loving ways we helped each other through tough times.

Spending quiet time reflecting alone or debriefing with each other after a difficult situation was tremendously helpful to us as a coping strategy. Many times this took place as we were going somewhere in the car. We could avoid interruptions and take the time we needed to catch our breath, make a decision, cry, or vent some frustration. It is much more difficult to carve out time to reflect in our current day of cell phones ringing at will. Turning them off from time to time is a necessary coping strategy in today's world.

My being kind to my spouse and his being kind to me were loving ways we helped each other through tough times. I can't really call this a coping strategy, but it definitely helped to receive or give a hug or go for a walk holding hands. Sometimes I felt so alone in dealing with Chris's mental illness that just knowing another human being liked me and was sticking beside me gave me tremendous support. The kind, caring moments between us became memories we could pull up for all the times when Rob and I were on our own with Chris and especially when I was alone after Rob died. Making a few sweet memories along the way is a coping strategy that families need to have in their bag of tricks for unexpected trials and hardships.

After Rob died, I sought counseling for myself. I realized that I was not just dealing with the grief of my husband's death and my son's horrific action. I was also trying to cope with a criminal justice system that I knew nothing about and that scared me to death. The stress of Chris's mental illness and poor prognosis erupted into an ominous horror scene of fear, anger, and helplessness. I began to feel overwhelmed with everything that I thought was expected of me. Then I got a letter in the mail from Baylor College of Medicine, Menninger Department of Psychiatry and Behavioral Sciences, asking if I wanted to participate in a research study to test the effectiveness of different counseling approaches for individuals over age sixty who were coping with anxiety and other mental health concerns. I had just turned sixty a few months earlier, so I called and asked if trauma and grief qualified. The program was free and I was in!

How My Faith in God Grew

As I have worked through the process of writing down my story, I've learned some new things about myself, even though my purpose was to help my readers learn something new about mental illness. Everyone faces problems in life. I had to face difficulties long before Chris's mental illness trapped us on the roller coaster. Because of that vicious, lethal ride, I learned that I can keep putting one foot in front of the other and taking one day at a time as long as God wills that I am still breathing. The coping strategies I used provided the mechanism that kept me going forward. Where did they come from? Through prayer and faith, I have leaned on God all along this journey. Sometimes I felt so angry and overwhelmed I tried to ignore Him and went about trying to prove that I

> I can keep putting one foot in front of the other and taking one day at a time as long as God wills that I am still breathing.

could fix my sick child by myself. Coping with chaos through my weak, human effort would never have been adequate. Later, after a few of Chris's suicide attempts, Rob and I developed this mantra: "Our job is to keep Chris alive!" We had no idea how much this pledge would cost.

Each morning God gives me a new day that He has made, and He tells me to be still and know that He is God. I did not see every day as God's when we were on our terrifying ride. But His days were there, and He placed blessings all around me. When I would look up from my veil of tears, I could see my precious grandsons playing in the sprinkler with my new puppy. One day while drinking coffee in my backyard, I was startled as a hawk flew right in front of my face. He landed on my fence not five feet away from me and perched there majestically for me to admire his profound beauty. I saw butterflies just sitting on my windowsill after I went through the terrible Hurricane Rita in 2005, shortly after Rob died. I had spent four days all alone in my house while everyone else in Southeast Texas was trying to evacuate to Dallas. The butterflies were a totally unexpected delight. Six weeks later I was in El Paso, Texas, attending a conference for my job. My hotel room was on the seventeenth floor. When I opened the draperies to look out the window, as I always do when I first go into a new hotel room, I was amazed at what I saw. It was a butterfly fluttering right outside my window. I said to my friend and roommate, "I didn't know that butterflies came to the seventeenth floor!" Then it hit me. Rob was with me in spirit, and God was alongside, bringing hope. He promised to help get me through my trials, not prevent them from happening. Being able to look back at all the blessings we had, despite the horror of Chris's mental illness, is a benefit that comes from taking time to reflect. I am much better at counting my blessings now than I was at the beginning of our ride. The blessings were there. I just didn't see them because I was so wrapped up in finding my own solutions. Silly me! God put helpers in my path, guided me to them, and gave me the courage and energy to learn something new and difficult every day. There were many times when I thought He was off helping someplace else and had left me all alone. Now, thanks to that high-flying El Paso butterfly, I know He was always beside me guiding my steps and helping me find my way.

Mental illness is a nasty element of this fallen world. Chris's illness was a horrible trial and hardship for my family, but I do not believe that God created this problem to punish me or entertain Himself by watching to see what would happen. God walked alongside of me to comfort and guide me. It is not important that I understand why Chris developed this terrible sickness just as he was about to become the adult person I hoped he would be. God's plan for each of us happens according to His timing, not mine. I trust Him to keep His promises. If God wants me to know the answer to the great "Why?" question, He will tell me someday. So far He hasn't, and I'm okay with that.

Now I am nearly always patient and calm. Few things really cause me significant stress. I do experience moments of anxiety, worry, or frustration. Others have hurt my feelings by something they did or said, but I automatically know I can't make that event disappear. My decision is either to address the matter if it is big or let it go if it is not. If my mind is so clogged with hurts and anger and fears that I keep holding on to, my vision of God's blessings will be blocked. I've learned to recognize these moments fairly quickly most of the time, and turn them over to God.

This hasn't always been easy! It takes practice. I must have been a hard case, because I've had lots of practice!

By the grace of God, here are my five most-used strategies in order of importance to me:

1. Seek God—grow my faith through prayer and study; give thanks for my blessings.

2. Seek professional help—learn and be willing to make changes; find a support group.
3. Rely on my team of family, friends, or strangers—let them lift me up, whatever my need.
4. Face reality—deal with it as it is; follow my instincts that have been sharpened by my past experiences with mental illness.
5. Find moments of quiet and reflection—be nice to someone else; do my favorite activity at least for a short time.

None of us is alone, despite how it may feel at times. God is waiting to put comforters and supporters in your path. Put your eyes on Him, and He will help you find your way.

22

Feet of Clay

The National Alliance on Mental Illness (NAMI) taught me that professionals may make mistakes, may misjudge a situation, and may even be swayed by a patient's persuasiveness. Like you and me, mental health professionals walk on feet of clay. No one is perfect. Attending NAMI meetings and hearing other families' experiences cautioned me to pay more attention to the details of Chris's treatment. The speakers at my support group and a NAMI conference I attended opened my eyes to other treatment modalities and convinced me that we were in for the long haul, likely the entirety of Chris's life. I knew a lot about mental illness because of living with it so long and having my professional training and job experience. Still, I realized I had a lot more to learn. I needed to learn how to become a mental health advocate in addition to being the parent of a son with mental illness. This may sound scary, but I am talking about being an advocate within Chris's treatment team. I was not sure that his treatment professionals were communicating with each other. That is the reason I began to write letters in late 2004 to his psychiatrist to ensure he was aware of what we as family members were seeing and to share what Chris's therapist and attending psychiatrists at the hospital were telling us as his parents. I always knew that my observations of Chris in crisis as well as when he was stable could be important information for his treatment providers to have.

I trusted the therapists, psychiatrists, and school psychologists who had treated and evaluated Chris for eleven years. I never contacted anyone who was not on our insurance panel. Insurance companies thoroughly investigate the professional credentials of anyone applying to be on their panel of approved providers. Also, if I had more than one choice of a medical provider, I would ask around for recommendations from friends and coworkers. I knew that mental health professionals had a code of ethics they had to adhere to, and their ability to practice and treat the public was governed by state licensing boards. When a psychiatrist has a case like Chris's, whose condition is refractory, or resistant to treatment, other professionals should be sought out for consultation. This was and is common professional behavior in all areas of medical practice. An ethical professional acting according to best practices will seek out colleagues for collaboration when necessary. I wish I had learned this much earlier in Chris's illness. I knew how to collaborate with my education colleagues and advocate for the programs that would meet Chris's educational needs. His time in special-ed classes and the alternative academic high school were his most successful periods during his teen years. For some reason I did not apply this knowledge and confidence in my association with Chris's team of psychiatrists and therapists. I shared as best as I could but credited them with knowing both the disease and Chris. I thought I just knew Chris as a parent, not as a mental health professional.

An ethical professional acting according to best practices, will seek out colleagues for collaboration when necessary.

When Chris was first diagnosed with schizoaffective disorder after breaking his neck in his suicidal response to auditory hallucinations, I knew his illness was out of my league. It takes my breath away even now when I think about all the ramifications of Chris being controlled by hallucinations and delusions. The psychiatrist who treated Chris in the hospital provided

Rob and me with an abbreviated graduate course in the long-term effects of psychosis. I don't remember how much he charged for his consultation with us that day, but it was worth every penny. We knew we had entered a new phase of Chris's illness and felt an even greater responsibility to understand and support his treatment. We needed to do everything we could to ensure his safety. At the time I never thought about the damage he might do to others but only the damage that was happening to him.

Mistakes in Chris's Treatment

I found many small errors in the huge stack of medical and legal records I reviewed before starting to write this book. Instead of stating that Chris had injected the stimulant drug ephedrine into his arms at age fifteen, one record said he had injected Excedrin. His age was listed incorrectly more than once, and one time he was identified as an African-American male instead of a Caucasian male.

Another record listed the date of the offense as June 5, 2005, instead of June 29. One record said I had asked Chris to walk the dog, and when I heard the dog yelp, I then asked, "Did you kick the dog?" My name was changed to Penny throughout another written document. None of these are significantly serious errors in terms of leading to a mistake in judgment, an issue of malpractice, or false accusation. But the fact is, mistakes are in the record. If they are in the record, then I know that the best-trained professionals are not perfect. They have clay feet, like all humans. I take this as a warning sign to be prudent and seek to understand when I am out of my comfort zone, whatever the situation.

There were three serious errors that I am aware of in Chris's treatment. The obvious one is that Chris intentionally managed to break his neck in a psychiatric hospital while on suicide watch. That was a stunning event. Many have asked why we did not sue the hospital. I don't really have a good answer to that question. I did talk to a lawyer after Chris returned home, and Rob notified the credentialing board of our insurance company, who conducted an investigation. But Rob and I decided to let it go. We did not have the drive within us to pursue a legal battle. If Chris had died, perhaps we would have gone forward, but the fact was, he lived and continued to be suicidal. We chose to reserve our energy for keeping our family and jobs intact and taking care of Chris to the best of our ability. Becoming involved in a lawsuit seemed like an activity for someone with leisure time on their hands. That was not us.

Becoming involved in a lawsuit seemed like an activity for someone with leisure time on their hands. That was not us.

A second error in treatment was one of omission. Despite how ill Chris was during his stays in Vernon State Hospital and while under the care of MHMRA in jail, no one sought out his previous treatment records. Between the ages of fifteen and twenty-four, Chris was admitted a total of thirteen times to psychiatric programs, including hospitals and intensive day-treatment programs, and all were because of suicidal actions, ideation, or serious self-harm. Four times he was admitted to medical hospitals for treatment of serious physical conditions that resulted from either a suicide attempt or self-harm. Before he killed his father, Chris had spent 295 days in the hospital for one reason or another, all related to his mental illness. In all the MHMRA and Vernon evaluation reports of Chris, only one suicidal attempt is mentioned, and that is the time he cut his wrists so badly that he ended up in Rusk State Hospital for almost three months. His broken neck, four-day coma from an overdose, abscessed arms, and the remaining times he cut his wrists are not part of his documentation anywhere following his indictment for murder. The Rusk records were readily available to the professional staff at Vernon because both hospitals are part of the state health department hospital system.

I am not critical of the treatment Chris received at Vernon State Hospital. In fact, it is the best treatment he ever received. I have great respect for the treatment plans and programs in place and the professionalism of the Vernon staff. However, I do believe that having specific details of Chris's previous treatment might have shortened his time languishing in jail. He might not have had to spend four months in a solitary cell with no medication and might not have become psychotic to such an extreme degree. I believe those four months of no treatment coupled with the awareness of what he had done intensified damage to his brain and mental abilities. The proof of my statement is seen in his poor response to good, consistent treatment during his first stay in Vernon following that initial four months in jail where he received no treatment or medication. From reviewing Chris's medical records at Vernon, I know he was much sicker there than he ever was prior to his dad's death, surely a culminating, disastrous event for Chris.

From October 2004 until Rob's death on June 29, 2005, Chris was seeing the same psychiatrist that he had started to see his senior year in high school in 1999. Because of Chris's frequent hospital stays plus his long stay at Rusk with follow-up outpatient treatment as an MHMRA client, this psychiatrist was not continually responsible for Chris's treatment during this six-year period. But he was Chris's primary provider of psychiatric care from 1999–2005 and the psychiatrist who knew us and Chris the best.

In the ten months of Chris's treatment prior to Rob's death, I believe the psychiatrist made mistakes in judgment in his treatment of Chris. I question whether he considered Chris's condition as severe as Chris presented. I wonder if he realized how many times Chris's medication had been changed over the years and how his stability was always so elusive. Surely he did since he had made many changes himself. When Chris told the psychiatrist that he had taken a friend's Adderall for a week and wanted his own prescription, why did the psychiatrist not recognize that as drug-seeking behavior, characteristic of a person who had abused amphetamines? I wonder if he ever reread and reflected on his own notes following a visit with Chris where he had described Chris as suspicious of others around him and cautioned Chris to "stop fighting with your mother." What did "fighting" mean to the psychiatrist—shoving me and his grandfather or just loud arguing? Did he read my letters to him those previous eight months about all the things that were happening at home? Why did he prescribe Adderall when I'd described Chris as a time bomb and the hospital psychiatrists had discontinued Adderall because Chris was psychotic? When he made the "egg on my face" comment in Rob's and Chris's presence at the June 23 appointment, did he not realize he was aligning himself with Chris and against us, his parents, who returned home after the appointment to endure another three weeks of Chris's terrorizing behavior?

Why the psychiatrist descided to prescribe an amphetamine to his psychotic patient is an absolute mystery to me.

The psychiatrist's failure to collaborate with Chris's therapist and the two hospital psychiatrists who had treated Chris in an acute psychotic state was a huge misjudgment, especially considering the outcome of his again prescribing Adderall to Chris. The behavior I described to him in my June 20 letter was not different than the behavior described in my other three letters. Chris's mental status had not improved. Why the psychiatrist decided to prescribe an amphetamine to his psychotic patient is an absolute mystery to me.

My Clay Feet

None of us in the Malone family was perfect. The coping strategies we developed over time helped us be more consistent and less reactive to Chris's behavior, especially when he was in a manic state. The weak link in our growing to fully understand his mental illness was that his symptoms continually changed, got worse, and constantly presented a new challenge to Rob and me. As parents we wanted Chris to be well! For a long time each little upturn, short period of calm, or spark of productivity at school would cause us to feel as if we had turned the corner toward recovery. Inevitably, we would let up on our close monitoring of Chris's medication. We would ask, "Did you take your medication?" rather than go into the kitchen and watch him take it.

At one point in our marriage, we seriously considered moving out of Houston to a less stressful environment for both of our sons. But Rob and I were living in a period of tough economic times. He had worked for big companies—National Steel, Western Company of North America, and Gulf Oil. All of them went out of business, shut down. Poof, and they were gone! We were wary of cutting ties to a place where we both had good jobs. We lived in the same house for twenty-four years. It was the only home Chris had known. We knew all the neighbors on our street. I don't know if not moving was the right decision, but we made a choice and worked to make the best of it.

At times Rob and I were overly sensitive to questions we were asked about Chris or what was going on in our family. Now I wish we had stiffened our backs and either answered the questions factually without emotion or had just remained silent and let the person think whatever he or she wanted. Instead, we tended to withdraw more into our own little chaotic world.

None of this seems terribly important to me now. The fact was, we were exhausted most of the time and became more and more isolated from friends as Chris's illness worsened.

23

Acknowledging My Losses, Counting My Blessings

Loss is a normal part of life on earth. If we are lucky, as children we experience small losses that are just big enough for us to learn that loss happens and we can recover from it. Learning to cope with small losses helps make a person able to handle bigger losses as they come along in life. The losses I want to acknowledge here are those I experienced as a result of the roller-coaster ride with Chris's mental illness. I suppose I was as prepared as most adults my age. My parents loved and provided for my brother and me to the best of their abilities. There was never any shortage of nurturing throughout my childhood. I felt ready for college, marriage, and the world of work when the proper time came. What I was not prepared for was parenting an out-of-control teenager, his mental illness, and the aftermath of a moment of psychotic rage.

When I look back, I realize that almost one-half of my adult life has been spent dealing with Chris's mental illness. I experienced many trials that seemed unbearable at worst and disappointing at best. A sense of loss followed many of these trials as they culminated in feelings of sadness, heightened anxiety, fear, confusion, ambivalence, shame, and grief. Some losses eventually moved to the back of my mind where they now rest quietly most of the time. Other losses screamed my name and took up residence in my heart as a result of the traumatic events surrounding Rob's death and Chris's arrest.

As the title of this chapter indicates, I will tell you about my blessings, after I describe my losses. I want you to know, dear reader, that I have coped, survived, and now live a full life despite the losses I've experienced. Counting my blessings has a lot to do with that. While the losses linger in the back of my mind and have left little holes in my heart, they no longer have the power over me that they once did. I'm not sure I would say that time heals all loss, but it does ease the pain, and on many days loss does not hurt at all.

When loss hurts now, I deal with it similarly to how I ease the pain I have from the arthritis in my hands. My favorite hobbies involve mostly handwork—quilting, drawing, writing, and gardening. If I wake up with stiff, swollen fingers, I do what I need to do to increase my flexibility and then go on enjoying what I love. This same process works for me when I wake up feeling sad, lonely, disorganized, or indecisive. I do what works to help me overcome those moments when loss flares up in my heart and mind. I reflect, pray, and contemplate the beauty of nature; in short, I count a few of my blessings. Then I do something, even if it is to take a day off to veg out and recover my energy from a particularly hectic few days.

Acknowledging My Losses

My first loss occurred when Chris began acting out at age thirteen and then continued to hone his negative, dangerous behavior to a sharp point. That first loss was the realization that the mental picture I had of Chris as a grown-up version of our cute, smart, sweet, creative young child would likely not come to be. I knew that even if he recovered from a "teenage rebellion," he was making some poor choices that potentially had long-term serious consequences for him. As a school counselor, I had met lots of kids who were strong willed to the nth degree and caused their parents a lot of grief. But most of them settled down in their early twenties—"late bloomers" we called them. With maturity they sought some education, landed jobs, and became responsible young adults. I hoped this would be the outcome for Chris, but it did not happen. I think all parents who have a child who is disabled in some way, is diagnosed with a serious or chronic childhood illness, or has suffered a major injury fully understand this particular sense of loss. At the same time we are hoping, believing, and searching for the best treatment, we have a nagging fear that we will lose the most important fight of our child's life. Thus, the fear gradually grows into a full-blown loss, which we parents grieve. The fact that this loss for me wasn't concrete and didn't have a specific date of occurrence that I could pinpoint on a calendar made it hard to recognize for what it was—something I could never change, something that would always leave me feeling sad, something to grieve. Chris would never be the adult man I had envisioned him to be. In fact, I didn't have a vision of him because I did not know if he would live to adulthood, and if he did, what would my role be with him? Would I still be a caretaker, encourager, financial supporter, or his first target should the mental illness run amok again? It will always be a confounding mystery to me, but I am sadder now for what it means to Chris to be diagnosed with a chronic brain illness that has no cure and has stripped him of his own dreams of a future.

Connection to Community

The rapidly ensuing events of Chris's dangerous manic behavior in eighth and ninth grades gave rise to other losses. On reflection, I see that two of these were logical losses based on what was happening on our roller-coaster ride. First, we lost our connection to community—spending time with friends, neighbors, church, and family. Our community connections became hospitals, psychiatrists and therapists, special education staff, support groups, and, of course, our jobs. Those connections, while human and interactive, were not satisfying. One of the biggest losses for Rob occurred when he lost his corporate job as an economist. It was a huge blow to his self-image as a good provider and protector for his family. A psychiatric hospital failed to protect Chris from breaking his neck in a suicide attempt while in its care, a huge loss of trust for me with the mental health profession. Then our collegial association with the special education team dissipated when in eleventh grade Chris and the assistant principal had the shoving bout over his hat.

> Much of the time I felt like a rubber band that had been stretched so far and for so long that I didn't have any stretch left.

An Overstretched Rubber Band

The second logical loss was the ability to bounce back from stress. There was little or no bounce-back time because the crises came one after another, and regular life just kept happening everyplace else around me. Our mothers got sick and died. Rob and I both experienced stress-related health issues that required major medical tests and multiple doctors' appointments. Changes happened in our jobs. We had hurricanes and tropical storms and weddings and graduations. Much of the time I felt like a rubber band that had been stretched so far and for so long that I didn't have any stretch left.

Mental Health Profession

Chris's treatment-plan failures also caused me to lose faith in my profession. I was effective in my position as an elementary school counselor. I'd always tried to form positive relationships with students, parents, teachers, and administrators. I implemented programs, conducted school-wide guidance lessons, conducted small-group sessions for students experiencing personal social issues, and counseled individual students in crisis situations. I was a good listener to teachers and gave suggestions for them to try regardless of whether a student was struggling with making friends or was being academically unsuccessful. Parents called me at school for advice when they were experiencing problems at home that were negatively affecting their child. I facilitated parenting classes at my school where parents could share ideas and learn new strategies from each other.

The frustration within me screamed. When my child was in desperate need of help, why couldn't the psychiatrist find the right medication? Why didn't all the school administrators know Chris's behavioral IEP and respond in a nonthreatening and de-escalating manner when a tense, provocative moment occurred? When my child was on suicide watch in a hospital, how could the staff not have intervened to save him from a broken neck?

My Daily Routine

A related loss which I fought and mostly overcame in my work was a loss of passion for my everyday personal responsibilities. It became difficult to get excited about my daily routine. I did not get excited about vacations, because we didn't take them. I did not get excited about a date with my husband, because we didn't have date nights anymore. I tried to get excited about decorating the house for Christmas, but it was often just another stressful period, especially with our mothers both dying at this time of the year. Having Christmas Day dinner with Chris at Rusk State Hospital did not feel much like the special family time this holiday used to represent for us. Being in crisis mode so much of the time kept me jagged up even when things were calm on the home front. I always felt driven and rarely took advantage of what downtime we had.

Shared Losses

There were specific losses that Rob and I shared. We lost the ability to have fun together as a couple. Will later shared this observation with me when he pointed out there had not been much fun in our lives. After Will was on his own as an adult, he said to me, "Mom, you need to learn to have more fun. You and Dad never knew how to have fun." After Will married and took on the adult responsibilities of home, family, and a job, his family often had friends over for burgers and football or some other family get-together. They take trips to the beach, celebrate kids' birthday parties galore, and go swimming, bowling, and to the movies together. On Friday evenings they often have family movie night upstairs, eat popcorn, and snuggle under afghans on the big old sofa. Nearly every weekend includes some kind of fun family activity. We grandparents take the grandsons for overnight stays periodically so Mom and Dad can have date nights. I am happy to see Will make this change in the way he conducts his family life. It is different from much of what he experienced growing up at home. In his teen years especially, our house was always serious. Psychosis had a way of taking fun out of our lives. That was a loss all four of us experienced.

Psychosis had a way of taking fun out of our lives. That was a loss all four of us experienced.

Loss of Intimacy, Two Views

Another loss Rob and I shared was a loss of intimacy. We were tired! All the time we felt bone tired. Sometimes we spent time "together," but usually we remained quiet and preoccupied with our own thoughts. After Rob died, the loss of intimacy took on a different meaning for me. In the last five years that we were together as a couple, I realize that our strongest bond of intimacy was built on our having ridden the roller coaster of Chris's mental illness together. We never differed in purpose. Our goal was to keep Chris alive. Rob and I did not have to explain our feelings to each other. I did not have to educate him on mental illness. I did not have to argue to convince him that Chris had an illness and that he was not just a mean, manipulative person. There is much more to intimacy than a physical relationship. What we had was akin to the popular guy phrase "I've got your back, man!" Trust. Protection. Knowing. Not judging.

Feeling Contented, Looking Forward

Tied to these two losses, fun and intimacy, was a loss of the sense of contentment, hopeful expectations, and looking forward to our joint future dreams. Rob wanted to own his own business. I wanted to improve my Spanish by taking a summer immersion study in Mexico. And we both wanted to take the family to Disney World for a dream vacation. I still hope to make it to Disney World someday with all four of my grandsons, and their parents, of course!

Concrete Event, Fixed Date

The greatest loss was inflicted on June 29, 2005. It is both a concrete event in my memory and a fixed date on my calendar. That puts it in the category of having an anniversary. The events of that day resulted in a compound loss that included death, physical assault, and chaos. I was filled with a sense of emptiness without Rob. It was almost impossible to get my mind around the fact that he was gone—dead, body buried, soul in heaven. To be "filled with a sense of emptiness" sounds like an oxymoron. How could I be filled and empty at the same time? After Rob's death even more losses seemed to pile on.

Loss of Self

My most overwhelming feeling at first after Rob died was the loss of a sense of myself. I could not fathom what was happening around me. I had trouble recognizing where I was. I lost my sense of time and the day of the week and all sense of a routine. The joke about walking into a room and immediately forgetting why I was there was no joke to me. That was my state of being, especially for the first few weeks. This is what I call my "numb period." It coincided with the trouble I had with getting garbage cans out to the curb, being continually late everywhere I went, and wandering the mall every night until I was either too tired to walk any farther or the mall closed. What I have discovered over the nine years since Rob died is that in early June, I always hit a down period. I live a very busy life, so I don't always perceive when a period like this is coming on. I've written about it in my journal and call it the "gray cloud." Just putting a name to it helps me cope with it when it arrives on the scene in the first week or so of every June.

I had the same experience when Chris was in jail for months and months before his trial. I went to all his hearings each month and usually did not expect anything significant to happen. I went on with life for three weeks following a hearing; then one week before the next court date, the gray cloud would revisit me. I would feel myself drawing inward—turning down friends for an outing because I did not want to leave the house, or picking a fight with Will over something like his forgetting to come by and put in new air conditioning filters for me. I would tell my friends that I would be fine in court without one of them coming with me. I felt as though I was imposing on them since the court dates seemed to go on and on without an end in sight.

But on one morning in particular, I did call a very close friend as I was standing in my closet crying while trying to get dressed. At the last minute I asked if she could go with me to court. She dropped everything immediately and told me to drive to her house. She would get dressed and drive us downtown. I pulled it together and at least got myself to her house. My friend took over the driving while I calmed down.

Back to Work

I experienced other losses that grew out of the major loss of Rob's death. When I returned to work after two weeks off, I quickly realized that I had lost my ability to focus and concentrate. I no longer could multitask as I had before. In the past I always had several projects going: planning a training session or monthly update meeting, revising sections of our counselor handbook, interviewing applicants for new and vacant counselor positions, serving on district-wide committees to coordinate events with other departments, responding to crisis situations at a school, or mediating disputes that reached the district level for resolution. I found that it was difficult to make decisions on the spot as was sometimes necessary or to quickly analyze and think through a problem. I could do it, but my confidence in the ability to lead, direct, and manage a large department had slipped.

The other thing that made this demanding pace, which I used to love, so hard to keep up with was that I had lost most of my energy. My get up and go was now wanting to move slowly and wander around a bit. I suppose you could say that my time-management skills were lost to me or even that

I was losing control of my job. In reality, I did not lose control of my job. I lost control of who I was at my core. Throughout my life I have always had an innate motivation and desire to help others. This was the area of training and education I continually sought out. This was my chosen career and my calling. With rare exceptions the stress I felt from my job had been good stress. In fact, the loss of the intensity I felt about reaching out and helping others played a key part in my decision to retire.

Thankfully, I was old enough to retire!

I lost control of who I was at my core.

Feeling Safe

In addition to losses I experienced in functioning professionally, I also lost my general sense of safety. Shortly after I returned home from staying at the hotel before Rob's funeral, a stranger came to my door one evening. I was home alone and had not yet gone back to work. It was not quite dark outside, but the sun had disappeared behind the houses across the street from me. I answered the door as I always had, and a young man about twenty was standing there smiling at me. At first I thought he was a solicitor, selling magazines or candy or restaurant coupons. After he greeted me, he said he just wanted to stop by and ask the neighbors about "violence in the neighborhood." I stared at him, told him I wasn't interested, and closed and locked the door. A full-fledged panic attack came on me. My heart was pounding out of my chest, and I felt totally weak. I was trembling and started crying. I didn't know what to do or what might happen next.

I phoned Will and told him what had happened. He asked if I thought it was an emergency. I didn't know if I had an emergency or not! Whom should I call for help? Should I just forget it and consider the stranger a cruel nut with nothing to do on a Sunday night? "Cruel nut" was Will's thinking, but he told me to call the constable if it would make me feel better. He wanted me to call him back to let him know what I had decided.

I did call the constable's office and talked with the dispatcher. I described my situation, including the fact that violence had taken place at my house a few days earlier. She consoled me but couldn't figure out what I wanted her to do. Finally she said she would call our neighborhood's extra-duty constable to ask him to stop by. The constable arrived a few minutes later and rang the doorbell. I was so glad to see him! I know he thought I was overreacting, but he listened patiently to my story and asked me to describe the man at the door. He then looked around the downstairs of my house holding his flashlight out in front as he walked into rooms where the lights were off. I was confident that there was no one else in the house but appreciated that the officer was trying to reassure me. He said he would keep an eye open for the individual as he cruised the neighborhood, advised me to lock my doors, said good-bye, and left.

I called Will back to tell him all was well. He was happy for me. The next day I started checking out the cost of alarm systems. One barking dog no longer gave me enough of a sense of security now that I was alone.

In addition to a new security system for my house, I also bought a new car. Having car trouble in my older car was something I did not want to face. The age of my house, almost thirty years old, also pushed me forward in the decision to buy my present, much newer house. I did not want to risk dealing with corroded, leaky galvanized water pipes, a hurricane-damaged roof, or appliance repairs that brought strangers into my house.

Forgetting Self-Care

Since I'd always had a caretaker-type personality, looking out for Benny was often on the back burner of my life. I did feel pleasure, contentment, and joy from helping someone else. In a way this was how I took care of myself. What shocked me about the loss of remembering to take care of myself occurred when I called my doctor's office shortly after my retirement to schedule my well-woman appointment. The nurse said she would try to get me in quickly since it had been so long since my last mammogram. I asked how long. She answered, "Three years." I didn't believe her! I had made these appointments every year. As much as I hated mammograms, I would never miss getting one, because we had a family history of cystic breast disease. My mother had had a mastectomy at age forty-five. How could three years have passed without my attending to this basic medical appointment? It turned out that my last well-woman appointment was just a few months before Rob was killed. Forgetting to make this appointment was representative of the sense of time, day, and routine that left me early on.

Counting My Blessings

I redefined my understanding of blessings during my four years as caretaker of my father-in-law, who was suffering from dementia, an illness which had no place to go but down. This is my new definition: *blessings*—everything good, from the tiniest to the greatest, whether it is good for the senses, the mind, the body, or the emotions. All good things come from God.

From this perspective it is easy to count the blessings I want to describe now—from our helpers with Chris, to my encouragers and comforters at Rob's death, to fair and compassionate legal minds, to dedicated, competent medical providers. The seventeenth-floor El Paso butterfly was a blessing. The hawk that sat on my fence was a blessing. My new puppy was a blessing. The births of my grandsons were blessings. The counseling research study letter was a blessing.

Learning to Have Fun

I credit my grandsons with teaching me how to have fun again. For the first time in twenty-five years, I bought a bathing suit and took the boys swimming at my neighborhood pool every chance I got. You do not sit on the edge of the pool when you take an eighteen-month-old swimming. I was definitely in the pool, remembering from my early-childhood training that water play is soothing.

The Kindness of Strangers

I only recently discovered another blessing that happened on the day Rob died. While in the middle of writing this book, I decided I should read the law enforcement reports from that day, June 29, 2005, as background material. I had avoided reading them before this. Those reports with their on-the-spot descriptions of what the police saw, heard, and did had not been something I particularly wanted to revisit. Nevertheless, I had a sweet surprise when I read that the first responders were also concerned for the welfare of our dog, Pepper, the one Chris kicked. One of the officers wrote that after all was done in the house for the investigation, he and another officer searched for Pepper. They found her hiding in the garage under Rob's workbench, one of her favorite places. They wanted to speak to a family member to ask what we wanted them to do with her since no one was at the house. But the only phone number they had for me was our home phone. They called the hospital, hoping to speak to me, but we had already left for the hotel by then, and the hospital did not know where we were staying for the night. The officers looked around my kitchen and found where I kept the dog food. They set out water and food for Pepper in the master bathroom and made sure that she was bedded down safely for the night. After asking Chris if he had kicked her, I never thought of Pepper again until I returned home four days later. Those officers were good to my dog nine years ago, and I appreciate their kindness toward all creatures, great and small, in the Malone household. No one was looking over their shoulders to make sure they did the right thing. They just did it. I didn't even know about their good deed for nine years. Will, Patty, Al, or the house cleaners must have checked on Pepper as well when they were at the house off and on the few days prior to Rob's funeral. But when I asked Will about Pepper after reading the police officers' report, he didn't remember anything about Pepper either. *Someone* took care of Pepper because she looked rested, well fed, and happy to see me when I came home.

The Prayers and Comfort of Friends

I still have a vivid picture in my mind of the many blessings I received from those who sent me cards right after Rob died. I received many, many cards, notes, and letters during the first few weeks. Some days my mailbox was stuffed. The postman probably wondered what had gone on with the Malone family. My dining room became my primary work area for dealing with post-funeral business. I sat at the dining room table and opened all the cards and read each one. I then placed them in a large shopping bag sitting in the corner of the room near my table. I did not disturb the shopping bag in its place in the corner until I moved out of that house two years later. By that time the cards were spilling onto the floor. When I was packing to move into my new house, I thought about getting rid of the cards. After all, they were part of the past, and I was trying to move into the future, starting over in my new house. As I started to stuff the cards into the bag, I reread a few of them. Once again I was touched and comforted by the words from my friends, just as I had been the weeks following June 29, 2005, when the cards first came in the mail.

I suddenly understood that those cards all represented prayers being sent heavenward on my behalf. That was a wow moment for me.

In addition to preparing for my big move, I was winding down my counseling sessions, which had caused me a lot of introspection. I suddenly understood that those cards all represented prayers being sent heavenward on my behalf. That was a wow moment for me. I literally envisioned prayers floating upward, an entire sack full of prayers. I remembered, that's how I got through those first months!

Again, blessings unknown to me at the time were a big part of my being able to put one foot in front of the other during my numb period right after Rob died. I went into my stash of shopping bags and retrieved another one big enough to hold the overflow cards. They all came with me to my new house.

Unexpected Blessings

Sometimes I got through hard times in unexpected ways, like being offered free research-study counseling when I most needed it. I count those times as blessings too.

It may seem like a strange blessing, but in God's infinite wisdom I did not see the blood on Rob's shirt. I can't imagine how seeing his back covered in blood might have intensified my fear and shock and perhaps interfered even more with my clumsy efforts to seek help when I called 911.

It was also a blessing that Patty's contact with a family member who was a lawyer, guided us to accept Chris's court-appointed attorney. Otherwise, we could never have gotten the quality of legal representation for Chris that he needed during a six-and-a half-year wait for trial.

My Inner Circle

Even now, one of the greatest blessings I continually experience is being able to reach out to people I love whenever I need to. I count three family members and a few very close friends as my inner circle. I can express just about anything I need to say or ask to my inner circle. Rough times still try to engage me from time to time, but my inner circle is always present for me. I do not have to be dressed well, speak articulately, or appear calm and wise in their presence. They know I am not perfect, but it doesn't matter. They love me. They like me. They know my story. Everyone needs an inner circle like this when trouble comes.

My inner circle does not necessarily always have a tough job. Sometimes a member's duty causes relatively minor interruptions in his or her life, but being willing to listen to my need is a huge benefit to me. When I was home alone one evening and still in our old house, I fell off a tall step stool and landed on my knee. It definitely hurt, and because no one was in the house with me, I felt not only hurt but scared. What if I had broken something and could not get up and walk to the phone? Falls can be serious for us seniors!

The old television commercial rang in my ears: "Help! I've fallen and I can't get up!" Fortunately, I had not broken anything, but I was hurt, crying, and upset. I called Will, who lived 150 miles from me, as I had a few weeks earlier when the scary stranger came to my door. I told Will about my fall and was trying not to cry. He was immediately concerned and asked me if I needed an ambulance, if I'd broken anything, if I was bleeding. After I assured him that I was okay and that I was just upset and scared, he got quiet. Looking back, I know what he was thinking. What was he supposed to do? He could not come over, have a cup of coffee with me, and help me calm down. We talked for a few more minutes, and he sympathized with me; he told me to be careful and to call him if I needed anything. I got an ice pack for my knee and sat down with my leg propped up while I thought about how many stupid things I do in life. And I vowed to be more careful on ladders and step stools. Logically, it was pointless to call Will in this situation, but emotionally I had to do it. I dealt with my emotional fallout first. Then I was able to take care of myself, thanks to the blessing of Will's sympathetic ear.

It was an important life lesson when I learned that it really is okay for Benny to ask for help.

Sometimes it is hard to ask others for help. *Self*-sufficiency and helping *others* had always described me. So it was an important life lesson when I learned that it really is okay for Benny to ask for help.

Part Six

THOUGHTS ON GOING FORWARD

24

Where I Am Now

First of all, I am happy to say that I am in a good place. I live fifteen minutes away from Will and his family. I have four precious grandsons, who bring me great joy. Chris is in the best place he could be, with no criminal case hanging over his head, and he has a dedicated treatment team concentrating on helping him recover his mental health. I still put one foot in front of the other and take one day at a time.

God is in charge, and His will for me continues to be revealed according to His time line. I have to pay attention to Him, so I pray and study His Word.

People have told me that they do not think they could continue to a have a caring relationship with the person who murdered someone they love as I loved Rob. I do not know how to fully respond to them. They may be right. Perhaps they would not ever want to know what happened to the killer; maybe they would always wish for the most severe punishment for him. Once I began to heal emotionally from the trauma of Rob's death at the hand of our son, I made a choice to forgive.

Chris is our son. He had a terrible illness that kept getting worse. Rob and I fought for his wellness, not out of duty, but out of love for our child. Chris is responsible for his actions, but he is not accountable, because his brain told him we were a danger to him, and his brain was wrong. Chris was a victim, just as Rob and I were. Chris trusted his own brain with all of its unbalanced chemicals and misfiring neurons. I can't imagine how that must feel, and I am so thankful for my own sanity.

I'm often asked if Chris ever felt any remorse. Did he ever say he was sorry for what he did? My answer is yes; Chris was devastated by what he did and continues to have overwhelming feelings of guilt. The first time I visited him in jail, the evening before Rob's funeral, Chris said about his dad, "I loved him. He was my best friend." I took that as an expression of deep sorrow. Later he penned a journal entry on the fourth anniversary of Rob's death:

> "6/29/09—Today, Dad has been dead for 4 years . . . I am sorry; I miss him. I destroyed my brother's plans for his children to know a good man, destroyed the twilight of my mom's life."

Medication may ultimately be able to stop Chris's voices and delusions, but it will not remove his sense of guilt. I don't know whether he will ever be able to forgive himself or know how these feelings will play out in his journey toward sound mental health. I will not ask God what He plans to do with Chris. I will only pray that He holds Chris in the safety of His loving hands.

The Nine Years, 2005 to Now

The short personal evaluation above does not tell you how I got to this state of mind. Furthermore, I don't know if, when, or how this current depiction of my life may change. I assume that I will have more trials—illness, natural disasters, more losses of people I love, accidents, financial challenges, or even random crime in my life. It is a fallen world. Bad things do happen to good people. This is earth, not heaven. This is not a new philosophy of life for me. I accept that trials and tribulation in life are eternal truths. Therefore, I do not feel bitter. When trials happen again to me, I will have a huge range of emotions, I'm sure, but I do not live my life as a bitter person.

This is what I have done, taking life one day at a time, since Rob's death.

Where I Am Now

- I worked three more years before retiring from thirty-four years in a professional career of education, counseling, and social work.
- I spent many months with lawyers, bankers, and CPAs taking care of immediate financial and legal matters.
- I hired a contractor and started work on fifteen years of delayed maintenance for my old house.
- I participated for ten months in Baylor College of Medicine's cognitive behavioral treatment counseling program with tremendous benefits.
- I got a new puppy and named him Buddy. He is a beautiful blue merle Australian shepherd who is protective of me and loves my grandsons as much as I do.
- I bought a new house and moved in.
- I put my old house on the market and sold it.
- I retired! June 30, 2008, was the big day, and it took months of planning for me to make that decision.
- The one thing I did totally for myself after retirement was join a weekly Bible study program. It impacted my life-after-Rob period immensely. It motivated me to make Bible study a priority in my life, and I began volunteering at my church in a program helping single mothers.
- Six weeks after I retired, my father-in-law had a sudden and complete fall into dementia. I became responsible for his care in an assisted living facility. I managed his financial affairs, including overseeing the rental and eventual sale of his house north of Houston, and I served as his power of attorney over finances and health for four years, until his death in 2012. I planned his funeral and said good-bye to the man who helped make my sweet husband the person I loved most in this world.

My father-in-law was ninety when he died, and I had known him for fifty-one years.

- My second retirement followed my father-in-law's death.
- I have taken four big trips with friends—my first cruise, New York City, San Francisco, and a driving trip through the Texas Big Bend country and New Mexico.
- I returned to my love of quilting and joined a quilt guild.
- I took up knitting and finally knitted a scarf, several in fact, though I have put it aside for now. It was my knitting group's "best knitter" who led me to serious Bible study—a double blessing!
- I took drawing classes and learned to observe shadows, shapes, and lines with my right brain.

Three big items on my list—going to my counseling sessions, becoming a serious Bible student, and taking care of my father-in-law's needs—stand out as being the most significant activities in my life's journey after Rob's death. They did not happen all at once but rather stretched out from mid-2006 to now.

Helpful Principles for Recovery

Participating in the counseling research study with Baylor College of Medicine came first. I was still working and had not yet retired. I emotionally hit bottom about ten months after Rob's death. I had made it through our thirty-ninth wedding anniversary, Thanksgiving, Christmas, my birthday, and his April 19 birthday. By that time I was struggling to get to work in the morning and to come home in the evening. I frequently roamed the mall after work until it closed, and then I would come home and fall into bed.

After completing many initial questionnaires and phone interviews for the counseling research study, I was randomly assigned to the cognitive behavioral treatment (CBT) group and began seeing a counselor. I had homework between my counseling sessions, which eventually curbed my mall wanderings. The counseling was hard work. I shed many tears and did some yelling, usually while driving in my car. The car continued to be a good place for me to vent and reflect, but on my own and without Rob.

One of the major issues I dealt with early on in counseling was how to characterize and remember the day Rob was killed. Should I remember it as the day Rob died or the day Rob was killed or even the day Chris killed Rob? In CBT jargon, that kind of thinking is called "all or none" and is considered a logical error in thinking. There was no rule, no one way to remember or describe what happened to my husband. I could say it however I wanted, which likely would be decided based on the circumstances I was in at the moment and who was asking the question. To this day, the CBT counseling strategies still provide me with a structure for reflecting, analyzing, and solving many of my daily problems and coping with emotional difficulties in a healthy way, both the big ones and the little ones. I learned valuable principles from my counseling experience.

One of the major issues I dealt with early on in counseling was how to characterize and remember the day Rob was killed.

Principle #1: Put yourself in capable, professional hands and fulfill your part of the bargain (which in my case was do my homework).

After my counseling ended, I knew I had to apply what I had learned: my new skills and my new insights about myself. The counseling was just the beginning of really moving forward. The most important thing I learned about myself through counseling was that I was experiencing a spiritual void to such a degree that I was almost paralyzed.

As I began to address this issue, I first bought a daily devotional book by Max Lucado. It became the start to my morning, every morning. I soon realized that I wanted a new study Bible to go with the devotional book because I wanted to understand the context of the scriptures that were cited.

I started journaling about my upsets, joys, prayers, and conflicts. I also included my observations in nature, which had always been a contemplative pastime of mine. What I encountered were surprising insights and patterns of behavior in myself and others. My counselor had told me, "Sometimes you just have to step out of your comfort zone in order to move forward. Go to church. Put yourself out there. People can't tell by looking at you that you've had tragedy in your life." I must have thought my shame showed like a dark light to the world.

I took her advice and started attending a new church. It was larger than my previous church, and I thought I could feel anonymous. This was very difficult for me. What I experienced were large crowds of strangers and God—all the things I had been avoiding and things that made me feel exposed, stripped, and emotionally naked. What kept me going was that I really liked hearing God's Word preached, singing songs of praise, and sharing in prayer. I admit I usually zipped out of the service as quickly as I could so I would not have to talk to anyone.

The resistance I continually fought in my seeking a way back to God did not disappear just because I managed to take myself to church once or twice a month. The next step I took to fill my spiritual void was prompted by a knitting group member. I'm sure I continued to be somewhat depressed, even though I no longer roamed the mall. Because my close friends were good listeners, I was able to safely express any down feelings I was having when our knitting group met. The best knitter in the group had told me previously about a Bible study class she attended on a weekly basis and really liked. Her husband had died of cancer several years before Rob died, so she knew about being on your own, grieving, and struggling to get past the sense of loss. Finally one day while I was moaning about something, she told me again about her class and said, "Benny, you just have to go!" She was so vehement that I meekly said, "Okay." She signed me up and I went. How many times did I hear this message in the year that our group of five novice and experienced knitters met? Many times! I learned another valuable principle.

Principle #2: Keep listening for God's message. He will repeat it if you don't hear Him the first time.

Starting this Bible study was the turning point for me. As with the counseling, I had homework every week. My void was getting smaller. I could feel it, especially as the study year came to a close after nine months of digging into the gospel of John. About midyear I told my small-group facilitator about Rob and Chris. Though it had been four years since Rob's death, other than my counselor, immediate family, and closest friends, she was the first person to hear the story from me. During this year of study in John, I also examined my own religious roots. This led me to a new knowledge and understanding of God's mercy and grace. I always knew that God loved me, but I thought I had to be perfect for Him, knowing full well that I absolutely could not be perfect. When that first year of the Bible study class ended, I began to see things differently through my adult eyes and was able to let go of a lot of my guilt and shame. There was a new principle for me, but it required faith for me to grasp it in my mind.

Principle #3: The peace that is not understood by people is real, and it comes from God.

When I began taking care of my father-in-law, Robert, shortly after I retired, I felt some resentment about having that responsibility thrust on me. Some of this feeling went back to my missing Rob. If he had lived, I'm sure that taking care of his father in his later years would have fallen on him as the oldest child and the one who lived nearest his dad. We already kept a close eye on him and made sure he was doing okay. Our primary concern in 2004 and 2005 was that he was becoming an unsafe driver, often the first dilemma of adult children taking care of an elderly parent. His dad of course thought he was perfectly fine, and we had done nothing but talk to him about our concerns. I was also tired, very tired after continuing to work for three years after Rob died. My job was consuming me physically and mentally. True, it helped me cope day by day because I was able to separate my work from my life's messiness. I was good at my job and loved my coworkers, but when I decided to retire, I knew it was the right time. I was so looking forward to making my own daily schedule.

I had a six-week break from work, and then my stress level shot straight up again. Will helped me move his grandpa into an assisted-living facility for memory care in his hometown so he could continue to see his regular doctor.

Several stressful things happened to Robert in the first few weeks of living in the memory-care facility. Within the first two weeks, he was hospitalized twice. He had a heart pacemaker implanted to stop the frequent fainting spells he started having after he moved to the facility. Next we had Hurricane Ike, which took direct aim at Galveston and raged north through Harris and Montgomery counties with its wind and rain. The memory-care center lost electrical power for several days as did thousands of homes in our part of Texas.

We got through the storm and encountered a few more medical and financial upheavals for my father-in-law, but within six months he had adjusted to the move, and I had a routine in place for his banking and bill paying, his rental property management, his clothing and personal item purchases, and his doctors' appointments. He and I had our routine too. I always took him out to lunch when we were together. Sometimes we would drive through his old neighborhood. Occasionally I brought his great-grandsons to visit on their school holidays, and Will would visit him on weekends. Grandpa always shared the big holidays either at my house or at Will's. But we quickly learned that his spending the night away was not good for him, because he would get confused in the middle of the night and could not remember where he was. Sometimes he did not recognize Will or me. I started picking him up just for the day and returning him before dark.

Robert began to call the memory-care facility home after about a year and a half of living there. After he had been there for three years, his physical health worsened significantly. I moved him to a new facility close to my house. The stress of the move and the new surroundings caused him to regress. Before his first week in the new facility ended, we had to make an emergency-room run on a Sunday afternoon because of complications with his diabetes. I knew it would be a blessing to have him so much closer to me, and that quickly became true. Thankfully, when I received the next phone call from the director of his facility at 5:30 a.m., I was able to meet the ambulance at the hospital in a reasonable amount of time. That became a frequent routine six months or so before his final decline.

Much of the time that I spent with my father-in-law during those four years he was lucid, and we had great conversations. He and Rob had very similar interests, and I viewed him as a wise man. He is the only person I ever talked to about my upbringing in the church of my youth. He understood and did not censure me for questioning the righteous rigidity of the belief system I grew up with. He'd had this same upbringing and come to view some of his own early beliefs as not in line with God's teachings on forgiveness, mercy, and grace.

When Grandpa was not lucid, he reminded me very much of Chris. He would become very distrustful and suspicious of others.

When Grandpa was not lucid, he reminded me very much of Chris. He would become very distrustful and suspicious of others. He thought someone was stealing his handkerchiefs or thought the staff had not come to get him for supper. He believed someone broke his phone when he had actually just unplugged it. He summoned the cable company several times to check his TV connection because he couldn't find the Houston Astros baseball games. He could not be persuaded otherwise, even after his caretakers and I made all kinds of systems of dry erase boards, calendars, and sticky notes to help him remember and understand. Like Chris, that part of Grandpa's brain didn't work the way it was supposed to.

The other thing I observed was that mounting stress and change were also Robert's enemies, just as they had been for Chris. I would sometimes see the same flash of fear-based anger in his eyes that I had seen in Chris's. I saw that it took him awhile to process information, and when he couldn't figure it out, he'd give a cliché answer. In other words he had a way of coping with his dementia that hid it from most people. He was a witty guy, and if you just saw him for fifteen minutes, you'd not know he had a brain illness. My father-in-law's way of covering his lack of understanding and memory reminded me of Chris's confusion when he was hearing voices that contradicted what someone was saying to him, such as the hospital note in Chris's medical record that said he "appears to be responding to internal stimuli." Chris coped by not telling anyone about his voices and kept his delusional thoughts to himself most of the time.

Another way Chris's mental illness and Grandpa's dementia were similar was that their behavior varied from periods of calm to demonstrations of anger, irritability, and rage. In the last six weeks before his death, Grandpa, a former bank vice president and trust officer, began shoving a certain male resident when the two were near each other. This man had been a police officer, and he would retaliate in kind and shove back. The two old men stood in a doorway pushing and shoving until eventually Grandpa punched the other man in the jaw. When the director called me that day to report this incident, I felt like the mother of a schoolchild receiving a call from the principal! It was not funny. The director told me that if my father-in-law became aggressive with the other residents, she would have to discharge him from the facility.

A few days later he started cursing and yelling that he had been kidnapped and was being held against his will. His ranting and stomping through the hallways went on for several hours and were disruptive. Two or three staff members walked with him, trying to calm him down as they dodged his feeble blows toward them. Eventually the director called me to come over and try to calm him down. When I walked in, I heard him yelling and walked over to him in the hallway. He stopped, stared in confusion, and asked, "Benny, is that you?" I said yes and hugged him. I asked him what was wrong, and he began to tell me about being kidnapped and held against his will. There was no doubt in my mind that he was angry. I persuaded him to go to his room with me so we could talk privately. I was able to help him calm down and encouraged him to rest on his bed while I talked with the staff. He stayed there for about fifteen minutes and then began pacing in his room, chanting like a teenage cheerleader, "Let me out! Let me out!" This kind of behavior came and went for several days with his doctor adjusting his medication and ultimately consulting a geriatric psychiatrist. I finally told the director to call the ambulance and take him to the hospital. My dear sweet father-in-law was experiencing the same kind of paranoid delusions that my son had experienced. And like Chris, Grandpa was becoming more and more dangerous to others as his brain illness became more severe.

My taking care of Rob's dad was what he needed and was an experience that also helped me. Even though it was not the life I originally had in mind, I became more patient living the life that was before me, and it became easier to notice the small blessings around me. What I had initially dreaded, I became content with.

I'm sure there are other blessings I do not know about, and I am thankful for them all. I discovered a new principle as I lived through the illnesses of my son and father-in-law. Two good men, one young and one old, lost the persons they had been because of a brain illness that distorted their perceptions of the world, disordered their thoughts, and sent their emotions on a rampage. This principle is valuable, not just for me but for all of us.

Principle #4: Brain illness is serious business for all of us and requires incredibly more research and study without regard to stigmatization of any particular form the illness may take.

Revisiting Counseling

Shortly after my father-in-law died, I decided to reenter counseling because the gray cloud paid a visit to me and would not leave. Although Grandpa's death was natural and expected, it was another loss for me. He and I had a special bond because of losing Rob the way we did—unnatural and unexpected. His passing also left me again without what had become a regular routine for me. Whether he lived in my house or in an assisted-living facility did not matter. I was still responsible for his well-being and felt less alone because of it. After he died, my feelings of loneliness started to turn into anger.

My old grief joined with my new grief. I was angry at Chris's psychiatrist and other professionals who had let me down in trying to help Chris. I was angry at the legal system for taking so long to bring Chris to trial. I was angry that the Vernon State Hospital was so far away. I was angry at Rob for leaving me.

Most of the things I felt angry about had happened eight to ten years ago. When I finally realized that, it stood out to me as a giant illogical thought, and my earlier cognitive behavioral training came back to me. I could stay angry and spiral down into depression, or I could get help retracing what I had already understood from my prvious experiences. It was a good decision.

Losses do not ever really go away, but you can learn some helpful tools to deal with them so you don't break down, fall apart, tremble in fear, or cry yourself to sleep every night. It is worth it to stay in one piece and still count your blessings each day.

Losses do not ever really go away, but you can learn some helpful tools to deal with them so you don't break down, fall apart, tremble in fear, or cry yourself to sleep every night.

25

A Broken System Cannot Heal Broken Minds

Many mental health professionals and advocates have characterized the mental health system in the United States as broken. The truth of this description is underscored by frequent news sources informing all of us of many specific examples of the system's brokenness. Rampage killings, family killings, and suicides by young men and women with severe mental illness are occurring too frequently and are widely reported. Their names are recited so often by the media that we can remember them—Andrea Yates, Jared Lee Loughner, James Eagan Holmes, Adam Peter Lanza. If we do not remember their names, we can recall what happened in their cities—Houston, Texas; Tucson, Arizona; Aurora, Colorado; Newtown, Connecticut. Perhaps names and cities escape you, but you remember schools, colleges, and universities—the Amish School, Virginia Tech, Oikos University, Sandy Hook Elementary. Maybe you remember killings that happened in restaurants—the Luby's massacre in Killeen, Texas; San Ysidro McDonald's shootings in San Diego, California; the IHOP killings of five National Guardsmen in Carson City, Nevada. Churches have also been sites of rampage killings—Wedgwood Baptist Church, Fort Worth, Texas; First Baptist Church, Daingerville, Texas; St. Jude Thaddeus Catholic Church, Albuquerque, New Mexico; Living Church of

God, Brookfield, Wisconsin. Mentally ill individuals were also responsible for mall killings in Oregon, Nebraska, and New Jersey. Killings by mentally ill psychotic individuals can and do happen anywhere! They touch the lives of all of us. And how many one-person killings by a psychotic individual, like Chris Malone's deadly stabbing of his father, do we never hear about? These numbers are undoubtedly recorded someplace in national and state databases, but these death lists reveal no face, no name, and no legacy of the grieving families left to mourn the tragedy.

Psychosis, the Enemy of Broken Minds

We must address our country's lack of an effective mental illness treatment system by facing the enemy, psychosis, the handmaiden of serious mental illness. Psychosis does the dirty work of schizophrenia, bipolar disorder, and major depression. Psychosis is no respecter of persons. It crosses all economic, social, racial, ethnic, and faith lines, and it has a penchant for attacking our youth first. Because psychosis is a potentially violence-causing, lethal brain condition, it poses a serious threat to public health and the safety of our country when left untreated or inadequately treated.

Psychosis does the dirty work of schizophrenia, bipolar disorder, and major depression. Psychosis is no respecter of persons. It crosses all economic, social, racial, ethnic, and faith lines, and it has a penchant for attacking our youth first.

How do we fight such a devastating brain illness? We fight psychosis and severe mental illness the same way we are fighting and have fought cancer, heart disease, birth defects, HIV-AIDS, and polio—with strong funding, research, public awareness, broad community support, and a coalition of committed leaders from medicine, research, private foundations, advocacy groups, and state and federal governmental entities.

Bringing the Brokenness Closer to Home

In retrospect it is clear to me that my son's psychosis was reaching a dangerous level in 2005 and that he was receiving inadequate psychiatric treatment. Until the fall of 2004, Chris had always hurt himself, never others, when he was depressed, manic, or psychotic to the degree that required hospitalization. It did not take a psychiatrist to tell me that his acting-out behavior was changing directions, with Rob and me personally experiencing miniattacks and continuous threats of harm. Chris had not been taking his medication regularly since returning home from the personal care facility at the end of May. Plus he was again taking a prescribed stimulant drug, Adderall, throughout the month of June. Rob and I had already learned three years earlier from the hospital psychiatrist when Chris broke his neck that psychosis can take up to a year or more to heal. That psychiatrist told us it was critical that Chris not deteriorate into psychosis again because each bout with psychosis damages the brain. Two hospital psychiatrists in 2005 essentially told us the same thing and took Chris off of Adderall because it was not the right drug for someone experiencing psychotic symptoms. That was the appropriate treatment for Chris.

However, after Chris was discharged from the 2005 hospital stay, his outpatient psychiatrist put him back on Adderall at Chris's request. Chris had been taking Adderall for twenty-seven days when he experienced the psychotic rage that resulted in my assault and his father's death. Chris was still in a psychotic state when the police arrested him at the house and transported him first to a hospital, then to jail, and finally to a state mental hospital four months later. His mind was broken, but someone else died as a result. I will always believe that Chris's treatment with Adderall was the ill wind that forced us off the roller-coaster tracks during our family's journey with his mental illness.

Mental Illness Isn't Always Psychosis

Psychosis is not an illness in and of itself, but if present, it must be treated aggressively. It results from an affliction of the brain and is symptomatic of a malfunctioning condition in the brain. The greatest publicity that psychosis receives comes when the media reports cases of violence caused by a mentally ill person having psychotic symptoms. Inevitably, the focus is on the motives of the perpetrator rather than on the existence of a severe brain illness. Often there may be some short-lived reporting about the inadequate mental illness treatment system in this country, but the conversation is soon replaced by talk of more gun control, stronger laws, and bigger prisons. Sometimes other societal issues, such as prayer in schools, loss of family values, or the need for better school systems, become part of the social media threads replacing discussion of the true issue.

The words *psychosis* and *psychotic* are used diagnostically in the medical profession. Not every person who experiences psychotic symptoms, regardless of the cause, displays violent behavior. Neither does every person experiencing mental illness become psychotic. Whether or not psychotic symptoms occur is more likely influenced by the kind of hallucinations and delusions that are inflicted on the person by the illness and the part of the brain affected by his or her condition. In Chris's case, his delusions were strongly paranoid and persecutory, causing him to feel threatened and in danger by people and objects, such as the radio, television, and other electronic devices. The voices that he heard, auditory hallucinations, continually reinforced his delusions by their persistently negative and bullying tone and by coming in powerful waves, which Chris described as "psychic hurricanes."

Not every person who experiences psychotic symptoms, regardless of the cause, displays violent behavior. Neither does every person experiencing mental illness become psychotic.

Some less severe cases of mental illness are successfully treated with short-term medication. Other cases may require medication and counseling, but eventually these treatments may be tapered off or reduced to a maintenance regimen as the person recovers. Lifestyle changes that reduce stress, eliminate alcohol and illicit drug use, and include the establishment of healthy sleep routines, nutrition, exercise, and a support network also contribute to and sustain recovery. In some cases, like Chris's diagnosis of schizoaffective disorder, the illness itself was considered intractable. In other words, whatever his treatment, nothing would have a significant long-term impact on recovery. Chris never fully stabilized on whatever antipsychotic medication he was taking, and mood swings kicked in before the psychosis healed. In the eleven years of Chris's treatment prior to his moment of psychotic rage, he was prescribed twenty-five different psychotropic medications and at times took as many as six medications on a daily basis. The dosages were frequently adjusted by his doctor in an attempt to find the magic balance that would not tip Chris into mania *or* depression *and* would control the psychotic symptoms.

In addition to severe mental illnesses like schizophrenia, bipolar disorder, and major depressive disorder, a number of other medical problems can cause psychosis, including

- alcohol and certain illegal drugs, during use and during withdrawal;
- brain diseases, such as Parkinson's disease, Huntington's disease, and certain chromosomal disorders;
- brain tumors or cysts;
- dementia (including Alzheimer's disease);
- HIV and other infections that affect the brain;
- some prescription drugs, such as steroids and stimulants;
- some types of epilepsy;
- stroke.[1]

Half of the eight causes of psychosis listed above are initially problems of the brain. How are schizophrenia, bipolar disorder, and major depressive disorder different from these other illnesses and medical conditions? They, too, are problems of the brain. The behavioral violence of mental illness, specifically psychotic rage, results after the brain becomes diseased and is not properly treated.

The Stigma of Mental Illness

In this highly technological twenty-first century with all its medical advances, I can't help wondering why mental illness remains a stigmatized, shame-creating disease that is surrounded by nineteenth century myths of demons and evil. Perhaps part of the stigma of mental illness results from a serious language usage problem. Mental health advocate and well-known psychiatric researcher E. Fuller Torrey, MD, takes this stance in his statement explaining the name change of the governmental entity now known as the National Institute of Mental Health (NIMH).

> The original name of the institute was to have been the National Neuropsychiatric Institute . . . The name change altered its essential function, from focusing on mental illnesses—diseases of the brain—to focusing on social problems thought to be relevant for mental health. Focusing on social problems inevitably led NIMH and its community mental health centers into political issues.[2]

Torrey further states that the needed services should not be "organized as mental *health* services" and then goes on to describe the "mental *illness* services" in other countries that he cites as having more successes than the American system.[3]

Words like *crazy, insane*, and *psychotic* are used interchangeably in the media as well as by the general public. According to Thesaurus.com, these words are all synonyms of each other in everyday usage. The word *crazy* likely originated in the sixteenth century from the word *crazed*, which referred to cracks or flaws in pottery glaze. Thus it has long been a vernacular expression used by people in general to describe someone who is acting or talking strangely.

Each of the other two words, *insane* and *psychotic,* has very specific definitions, one legal and one medical. When judges, lawyers, psychiatrists, and psychologists use *insane* and *psychotic* together, they are usually referring to a seriously ill individual with a history of mental illness who has no sense of right or wrong and who has committed a violent crime.

In my son's case I saw and understood that his intermittent rants about being either God or Satan were manifestations of his hallucinations and delusions. He was definitely capable of violence during these psychotic episodes, but the violence came out of a brain illness and not from an evil spirit's possession of his mind and body.

The importance of communicating the right message with our language was underscored in a recent statement by Thomas Insel, MD, director of NIMH. Believing a "rethink" is in order, he stated, "Deaths from medical causes such as leukemia and heart disease have decreased over the past thirty years. The same cannot be said of the suicide rate, which has remained the same. A vast majority of suicides—90 percent—are related to mental illness such as depression and schizophrenia." He further stated, "We need to think of these as brain disorders" rather than referring to them as "a mental or behavioral disorder." He cites research that "indicates that mental illness may be more of a neuronal connection or circuit disorder. The earlier these circuits are identified, the earlier preventive treatments could be used to save the lives of people with mental illnesses." To emphasize the importance of "preventive treatments," Insel offered the following comparison: "If we waited for the 'heart attack,' we would be sacrificing 1.1 million lives every year in this country. That is precisely what we do today when we decide that everyone with one of these brain disorders, brain circuit disorders, has a behavior disorder. We wait until the behavior emerges. That's not early detection; that's not early prevention." The behavior that emerges in the form of psychotic rage can unfortunately result in death and injury to many individuals, not just the person with the mental illness. Brain disorder, brain disease, brain illness, brain circuit disorder—we do have better language, and we need to start using it.[4]

How long will it be before families of persons with severe mental illness can read a headline like the one below, which parents of children with leukemia were able to read recently?

Childhood Leukemia Survival Rates Improve Significantly

> A new study shows that children with the most common type of childhood cancer, acute lymphoblastic leukemia (ALL) have a survival rate of more than 90 percent.[5]

Compare the data cited by Insel (2013) that 90 percent of suicides are related to severe mental illness to this statistic regarding the significantly improved childhood leukemia survival of rate 90 percent reported above. We can only hope that in not too many years a family with a twenty-something son or daughter who is diagnosed with a severe mental illness will be able to read such a promising, though currently fictional, headline as the one below:

New Treatment for Psychotic Symptoms Results in Significant Reduction in Homicidal and Suicidal Ideation in Persons with Severe Mental Illness

26

A Look at New and Promising Initiatives

The experts in mental illness—families, researchers, mental health professionals, and advocates—know that successful treatments are out there. We are always looking for ways to push forward scientific knowledge that can enhance discovery, development, and implementation of promising advances in the treatment of mental illness. An important part of our mission is to share what is new and promising in hopes that good will come to the target population—individuals and families coping with mental illness.

While I had a head start in being trained to advocate for Chris's treatment needs because of my education and choice of career, the vast amount of my knowledge on how and what to say to his treatment team members was gained after getting on the roller coaster of his mental illness journey. Now the information available to us regarding hopeful avenues for going forward is often just a click away. Access to a computer and the Internet is all you will need to start yourself out on the path to becoming a confident mental health advocate.

Even now I still want to know and understand more about the complexities of Chris's illness. He still is ill but doing well in a protected treatment environment, yet I do not know what the future holds for him. Our story is not finished. Each new discovery I read about that offers potential for his recovery gives me hope and encouragement. I hope you find the same as you seek to learn more about this illness that is such a mystery.

What Is Out There?

Some of the initiatives described below were experienced by my family during our time of dealing with Chris's illness, and I found them to be valuable. Others I can only look at and wish they had been available as an option for Chris.

Early Psychosis Prevention

Chris's illness had its origins in his teen years, a pattern that is common and supported by research. Early diagnosis and treatment of any illness enhances the possibility of a more favorable outcome for the person with the illness. While we did seek counseling early in his onset of bipolar disorder, we missed understanding the symptoms of psychosis and acting on that quickly. Programs that emphasize effective early detection and treatment of psychosis and mental illness can yield lifelong benefits for the young person experiencing this emerging illness. One promising new program is the Portland [Maine] Identification and Early Referral (PIER) program. Established in 2001 as a prevention system for identifying and treating youths at high risk of an initial psychotic episode, this very promising model is now being replicated in other cities in the United States (*www.piertraining.com/pier-model*, accessed 1/1/2014). A list of the fifteen early psychosis prevention and intervention clinics in the United States can be found at *www.schizophrenia.com/earlypsychosis.htm* (accessed 1/20/2014).

Technological Applications

Coping with Voices, developed by Cognitive Health Innovations, Inc., is a new software available to help teach coping strategies to people with schizophrenia. It is a new clinically tested, self-help program that is based on cognitive behavioral therapy. Intended to be only one element of a person's treatment plan, its counseling approach addresses the symptom of auditory hallucinations and voices and helps the person begin developing effective coping strategies (*www.piertraining.com/pier-model*, accessed 1/1/2014).

PTSD Coach is a free mobile app both for Android and iPhones that was designed for veterans and military service members who have, or may have, posttraumatic stress disorder (PTSD). This app provides users with education about PTSD, information about professional care, a self-assessment for PTSD, opportunities to find support, and tools that can help users manage the stresses of daily life with PTSD. Tools range from relaxation skills and positive self-talk to anger management and other common self-help strategies. Users can customize tools based on their preferences and can integrate their own contacts, photos, and music. *PTSD Coach* was created by the US Department of Veterans Affairs National Center for PTSD and the Department of Defense's National Center for Telehealth & Technology (*www.ptsd.va.gov/public/materials/apps/PTSDCoach.asp*, accessed 1/31/2014.

Assertive Community Treatment

A NAMI fact sheet on assertive community treatment (ACT) describes this approach as a multidisciplinary team model of services for providing community-based treatment for the most severely mentally ill persons (*www.nami.org/factsheets/ACT_factsheet.pdf*, accessed 1/23/2014). The treatment, support, and rehabilitation services provided are individualized, flexible, and comprehensive in nature. This type of program has been lauded for its cost effectiveness, and research has shown it to be successful in helping individuals with the greatest needs, especially those who have not been helped by other services. The Assertive Community Treatment Association website is another good source of information about this treatment model (*www.actassociation.org*, accessed 1/23/2014).

Clubhouse for Psychosocial Rehabilitation

A supportive element of treatment is the "clubhouse" model. Clubhouses provide a day program of psychosocial rehabilitation for individuals with severe and persistent mental illnesses. Participants are called members rather than clients or patients, and joining a clubhouse program is strictly voluntary. The goal of the program is to contribute to the recovery of individuals through the use of a therapeutic environment that includes responsibilities within the clubhouse, as well as support for outside employment, education, meaningful relationships, housing, and an overall improved quality of life.

The first clubhouse opened in 1948 in New York. More information is available on the website of International Center for Clubhouse Development, referred to as Clubhouse International (*www.iccd.org/whatis.html*, accessed 1/24/2014).

Affordable Housing

Since a large number of homeless persons have a severe mental illness, federal housing policies impacting homelessness need to be linked to Health and Human Services policies regarding treatment for the mentally ill, a recommendation made by the Johns Hopkins Institute for Policy Studies in a recent analysis of these two related social problems (*http://ips.jhu.edu/pub/The-Severely-Mentally-Ill-Homeless-Housing-Needs-and-Housing-Policy*, accessed 1/23/2014).

In Houston, Texas, the Mental Health Mental Retardation Authority of Harris County (MHMRA) in 2012 developed the Acres Homes Garden Apartments as permanent, affordable housing for persons with schizophrenia, bipolar disorder, and major depressive disorder who also have financial need. There are now 100 such housing units in Harris County. But the most recent statistics from the Coalition for the Homeless reveal that between fifteen hundred and two thousand individuals are chronically homeless in Harris County, and many in this population are severely mentally ill. The need for housing that is safe and permanent and affordable greatly exceeds its availability in this large Texas metropolitan area (*www.homelesshouston.org/wp-content/uploads/2013/06/FINAL-PIT-2013-Release.pdf*, accessed 1/23/2014).

School Mental Health Project

Another promising program that provides an avenue for early intervention among students is the School Mental Health Project. Research studies conclude that as few as one-sixth to one-third of youth with diagnosable mental illness receive any treatment, and of those who do, less than half receive adequate treatment. Such programs are collaborative efforts involving schools, parents, and community mental health agencies, which come together to address students' educational, emotional, and behavioral needs.

The American Academy of Pediatrics supports school-based mental health programs because of the strong potential they offer for prevention as well as intervention in meeting the mental health needs of children and adolescents. In the Pediatric Academy's policy statement, specific recommendations are offered to support the goal that primary health care professionals, mental health providers, and educators work in close collaboration to develop and implement effective services within schools (*Journal of Abnormal Child Psychology*, 33, no. 6, December 2005): 657–63. *http://gucchdtacenter.georgetown.edu/resources/Call%20Docs/2010Calls/paternite_sbmhOverview2005.pdf*, accessed 1/24/2014).

Jail Diversion Practices

In an attempt to understand the scope of the problem of mentally ill offenders in the criminal justice system, a recent study (2010) was conducted by the Treatment Advocacy Center and the National Sheriffs' Association. The title of the study report reveals its primary findings: "More Mentally Ill Persons Are in Jails and Prisons Than Hospitals: A Survey of the States." The report states that there are more than three times the number of seriously mentally ill persons in jails and prisons than there are in hospitals (*www.treatmentadvocacycenter.org/storage/documents/final_jails_v_hospitals_study.pdf*, accessed 1/24/2014).

New approaches that are being tried are called diversion practices and are designed to keep severely mentally ill, nonviolent offenders involved in treatment programs rather than housed in crowded jails and prisons. Some of the diversion programs that are showing success include:

- Crisis Intervention Team policing, which relies on specially trained officers to respond to mental illness–related calls (*Catalyst*, A Newsletter from the Treatment Advocacy Center, Fall 2013).

- Special jail units for mentally ill offenders, which separate mentally ill inmates from the regular jail population and allow the administration of individually prescribed psychotropic medications and medical supervision by forensic mental health professionals working in the jail setting (*www.texasobserver.org/want-treatment-mental-illness-go-to-jail/*, accessed 1/26/2014).

- Mental Health courts, which allow qualifying criminal defendants to receive community-based mental health treatment (*Catalyst*, Fall 2013)

- Assisted outpatient treatment (AOT), which requires a person to comply with a court order to participate in outpatient treatment and take prescribed medication as a condition for living outside the hospital (*American Psychosis*, Torrey, p. 147).

- Conditional release, which is similar to AOT but with the exception that the judicial authority is vested in the psychiatric hospital's executive director (*American Psychosis*, Torrey, p. 147).

- My own community of Harris County, Texas, approved a plan to establish a Felony Mental Health Court on November 19, 2009. The idea was to ensure that a mentally ill defendant receives treatment while under close supervision of the court, with the hope that those who are mentally ill will no longer cycle in and out of jail unnecessarily as they make progress in responding to treatment (*http://app1.kuhf.org/articles/1355703857-First-Year-Of-Harris-County-Mental-Health-Court-Gets-Good-Review-From-Judge.html*, accessed 1/25/2014).

Mental Health Programs for Veterans

The Veterans Health Administration (VHA) has focused efforts on reducing the suicide rate among veterans. A 2014 update report revealed that the suicide rate for male VHA users remains considerably higher than the general US male population. However, in an older age bracket, male VHA users' suicide rates have actually decreased while US male suicide rates in the same age bracket have increased. One promising initiative to help reduce the suicide rate among veterans is the establishment of Psychosocial Rehabilitation and Recovery Centers, which enhance traditional mental illness treatment by adding a life-adjustment component. The program is completely voluntary and offers classes and activities to help veterans with a serious mental illness build social skills, learn to effectively manage their symptoms, and integrate back into the community. Both professional mental health staff and peer support volunteers assist the veterans in moving forward toward a more fulfilling life (*www.mentalhealth.va.gov*, accessed 1/26/2014).

National Dialogue on Mental Health

Following the Newtown, Connecticut, rampage killings in December 2012, President Obama issued a four-point plan to address the horrific killings that took place at Sandy Hook Elementary School. The plan is entitled "Now Is the Time: The President's Plan to Protect our Children and Our Communities by Reducing Gun Violence." Two of the plan's steps address the problems of (1) guns in dangerous hands and (2) military-style assault weapons and high-capacity magazines. The remaining two steps focus on (3) making schools safer and (4) increasing access to mental health services. In a speech on June 3, 2013, before the White House National Conference on Mental Health, President Obama charged the secretaries of the federal departments of Health and Human Services and Education to launch National Dialogue on Mental Health, an outreach program that aims to educate citizens about mental health issues and to develop strategies to reduce the stigma associated with mental illness, thus finally eliminating the major barrier to seeking treatment (*www.nimh.nih.gov/about/director/2013/a-national-dialogue.shtml*, accessed 1/27/2014).

As a result of President Obama's "Now Is the Time" plan, many governmental, educational, and medical entities and organizations as well as private mental health advocacy groups have joined the campaign to bring more public awareness to the issues of mental illness. Resources for education and treatment, recommendations for addressing the huge problem of severe mental illness and psychosis, and initiatives for diminishing the stigma of mental illness by attacking myths and replacing them with facts are readily available. To encourage the greatest study of this topic, many mental health websites and publications offer additional links for information and resources. The information available today, compared to what was available to me in the eleven years leading up to June 29, 2005, is immensely greater. Searching different websites now I find a unity of purpose of all the groups who want to respond to the call to action to find solutions that will help prevent events like the one at Sandy Hook Elementary School on December 14, 2012.

To learn more about the National Dialogue on Mental Health, including how you can participate, visit *www.CreatingCommunitySolutions.org*. The Substance Abuse and Mental Health Services Administration (SAMHSA) has developed helpful resources for advocacy. The Toolkit for Community Conversations About Mental Health is designed to be a resource to help those interested in holding a community dialogue about mental health and is available for free on the SAMHSA website (*www.samhsa.gov/communityconversations,* accessed 1/29/2014).

Finally

I hope this call to action and America's response will also find solutions for families like mine, and perhaps yours, whose loved one died unnecessarily as a result of his child's severe mental illness. I hope we will someday read my imaginary headline below and it no longer will be imaginary. It will be true!

**New Treatment for Psychotic Symptoms Results in
Significant Reduction in
Homicidal and Suicidal Ideation in Persons with Severe Mental Illness**

Faith, hope, and encouragement keep me going—one step at a time, one day at a time. I wish the same for you.

APPENDIX OF HELPFUL RESOURCES

Websites, Videos, and Publications

Support Networks for Individuals, Families, Communities

Action Alliance for Suicide Prevention—The purpose of this organization is to advance the National Strategy for Suicide Prevention (NSSP). NSSP is the first attempt in the United States to prevent suicide through a systematic approach. It lays out a framework for developing an array of suicide prevention services and programs. At all levels of government as well as in the private sector, the NSSP emphasizes coordination of resources and the application of culturally appropriate services (*www.actionallianceforsuicideprevention.org*).

American Foundation for Suicide Prevention—The AFSP is the nation's leading organization bringing people together across communities and backgrounds to understand and prevent suicide and to help heal the pain it causes. Individuals, families, and communities who have been personally touched by suicide are the moving force of this organization (*www.afsp.org*).

Mental Health Grace Alliance—Mental Health Grace Alliance is a faith-based, non-profit organization created to promote understanding in the church and provide assistance and support to individuals living with mental illness and their families (*http://arborteam.wix.com/mhgracealliance#!*).

Creating Community Solutions—This organization is an important part of the National Dialogue on Mental Health. Its purpose is to give Americans a chance to learn more about mental health issues from research and from each other (*wwwcreatingcommunitysolutions.org/national-dialogue-mental-health*).

Healthyplace.com—This is the largest consumer mental health site on the Net. It provides authoritative information and support to people with mental health concerns, along with their family members and other loved ones (*www.healthyplace.com*).

International Bipolar Foundation—This is a not-for-profit organization based in San Diego whose mission is to improve understanding and treatment of Bipolar Disorder through research; to promote care and support services for individuals and caregivers; and to erase associated stigma through education *(http://www.ibpf.org/).*

Mental Health America—MHA is a leading advocacy organization addressing the full spectrum of mental and substance use conditions and their effects nationwide. It works to inform, advocate, and enable access to quality behavioral health services for all Americans (*www.mha.net*).

National Alliance on Mental Illness—NAMI is the nation's largest grassroots mental health organization dedicated to building better lives for the millions of Americans affected by mental illness. NAMI advocates for access to services, treatment, support, and research and is steadfast in its commitment to raise awareness and build a community of hope for all those in need (*www.nami.org).*

Schizophrenia.com—This community-oriented website provides in-depth information, support, and education about schizophrenia and related disorders (*www.schizophrenia.com*).

Treatment Advocacy Center—This nonprofit organization is dedicated to eliminating barriers to the timely and effective treatment of severe mental illness. The organization promotes laws, policies, and practices for the delivery of psychiatric care and supports the development of innovative treatments for and research into the causes of severe and persistent psychiatric illnesses, such as schizophrenia and bipolar disorder (*www.treatmentadvocacycenter.org*).

Scientific and Medical Information

Healthychildren.org and **American Academy of Pediatrics** (AAP)—These companion websites provide information for parents on physical, mental, and social health and well-being for infants, children, adolescents, and young adults. Both specific and general guidance topics are offered on these websites and through publications of the AAP (*www.healthyplace.com* and *www.aap org*).

Schizophrenia Research Forum—The Schizophrenia Research Forum website is sponsored by the Brain and Behavior Research Foundation and was created with funding from the US National Institute of Mental Health (*www .schizophreniaforum.org/new/detail.asp?id=1997*).

WebMD—This site provides health information on specific topics, including mental health, and offers a safe forum where you can create or participate in support groups and discussions about health topics that interest you (*www .webmd.com/mental-health/default.htm*).

Governmental Websites on Mental Health

MedlinePlus—This website is produced by the National Library of Medicine, part of the National Institutes of Health. It provides free information about diseases, conditions, and wellness issues and offers reliable, up-to-date health information (*www.nlm.nih.gov/medlineplus/mentaldisorders.html*).

MentalHealth.gov—This site shares mental health information, including signs of mental health problems, ways to talk about it, and getting help (*www.mentalhealth.gov*).

Myths and Facts—This excellent document provides understanding of the scientific basis of mental illness and related issues and is a valuable tool for advocacy purposes. This document appears at end of the chapter (*www.MentalHealth.gov/basics/myths-facts/index.html*).

National Institute of Mental Health—NIMH, part of the National Institutes of Health, is the largest scientific organization in the world dedicated to research focused on the understanding, treatment, and prevention of mental illness. Its goal is to provide a framework to focus and accelerate mental health research so that breakthroughs in science can be utilized to tangibly improve mental health care and the lives of people with and affected by mental illness (*www.nimh.nih.gov*).

Substance Abuse and Mental Health Services Administration—The SAMHSA agency is within the US Department of Health and Human Services that leads public health efforts to advance the behavioral health of the nation. SAMHSA's mission is to reduce the impact of substance abuse and mental illness on America's communities (*www.samhsa.gov*).

The White House—This helpful site provides information on presidential efforts concerning mental health issues, including copies of speeches and executive documents (*www.whitehouse.gov*).

Schizophrenia Videos Available on YouTube

1. "I Hear Voices: A Story on Schizophrenia." Learn more about schizophrenia on this video, filmed in Singapore. *http://youtube/KBRA-C4acr70*, 5:53 minutes. Uploaded on February 9, 2012.
2. "Janssen Pharmaceuticals: Schizophrenia Simulation." *http://youtube/T14neSm599g*, 4:31 minutes. Uploaded on June 17, 2010.
3. "My Schizophrenia Experience." Video by twenty-year-old man describing his life with disorganized schizophrenia. *www.youtube.com/watch?feature=player_detailpage&v=xuyG_YeQiu0*, 21:04 minutes. Published on March 29, 2013.
4. "Schizophrenia Simulated." A simulation of what it is like to live with schizophrenia. *http://youtube/KYHVbLLO2bU*, 5:18 minutes. Published on January 8, 2013.
5. "Schizophrenic Simulation: What my voices sound like when I am without medication for a week or so." *http://youtube/zMxD8RV3n8E*, 34 seconds. Uploaded on December 5, 2010.
6. "Sounds of a Mental Illness." *http://youtube/_oD4QxTjExs*. 6:53 minutes. Published on April 24, 2013.

Publications

Duke, Patty, and Gloria Hochman. *A Brilliant Madness: Living with Manic-Depressive Illness*. New York: Bantam Books, 1992.

Greek, Milt. *Schizophrenia: A Blueprint for Recovery*. Athens, Ohio: Milt Greek, Publisher, 2012.

Gur, Raquel E., and Ann B. Johnson. *If Your Adolescent Has Schizophrenia: An Essential Resource for Parents*. New York: Oxford University Press, 2006.

Jamison, Kay R. *An Unquiet Mind: A Memoir of Moods and Madness*. New York: Alfred A. Knopf Inc., 1995.

Ross, Marvin. *Schizophrenia: Medicine's Mystery-Society's Shame.* Dundas, Canada: Bridgeross Communications Inc., 2008.

Snyder, Kurt, Raquel E. Gur, and Linda W. Andrews. *Me, Myself, and Them: A Firsthand Account of One Young Person's Experience with Schizophrenia.* New York: Oxford University Press, 2007.

Torrey, E. Fuller. *American Psychosis: How the Federal Government Destroyed the Mental Illness Treatment System.* New York: Oxford University Press, 2014.

———. *Surviving Schizophrenia: A Manual for Families, Consumers, and Providers,* 6th ed. New York: Harper Collins Publishers, 2006.

Woolis, Rebecca. *When Someone You Love Has a Mental Illness.* New York: Penguin Group, 2003.

Mental Health Myths and Facts

Can you tell the difference between a mental health myth and fact? Learn the truth about the most common mental health myths.

Mental Health Problems Affect Everyone

Myth: Mental health problems don't affect me.
Fact: Mental health problems are actually very common. In 2011, about:

- One in five American adults experienced a mental health issue;
- One in 10 young people experienced a period of major depression;
- One in 20 Americans lived with a serious mental illness, such as schizophrenia, bipolar disorder, or major depression.
- Suicide is the 10th leading cause of death in the United States. It accounts for the loss of more than 38,000 American lives each year, more than double the number of lives lost to homicide.

Myth: Children don't experience mental health problems.
Fact: Even very young children may show early warning signs of mental health concerns. These mental health problems are often clinically diagnosable, and can be a product of the interaction of biological, psychological, and social factors.

Half of all mental health disorders show first signs before a person turns 14 years old, and three quarters of mental health disorders begin before age 24.

Unfortunately, less than 20 percent of children and adolescents with diagnosable mental health problems receive the treatment they need. Early mental health support can help a child before problems interfere with other developmental needs.

Myth: People with mental health problems are violent and unpredictable.
Fact: The vast majority of people with mental health problems are no more likely to be violent than anyone else. Most people with mental illness are not violent and only 3–5 percent of violent acts can be attributed to individuals living with a serious mental illness. In fact, people with severe mental illnesses are over ten times more likely to be victims of violent crime than the general population. You probably know someone with a mental health problem and don't even realize it, because many people with mental health problems are highly active and productive members of our communities.

Myth: People with mental health needs, even those who are managing their mental illness, cannot tolerate the stress of holding down a job.
Fact: People with mental health problems are just as productive as other employees. Employers who hire people with mental health problems report good attendance and punctuality as well as motivation, good work, and job tenure on par with or greater than other employees.

When employees with mental health problems receive effective treatment, it can result in:

- Lower total medical costs
- Increased productivity
- Lower absenteeism
- Decreased disability costs

Myth: Personality weakness or character flaws cause mental health problems. People with mental health problems can snap out of it if they try hard enough.
Fact: Mental health problems have nothing to do with being lazy or weak, and many people need help to get better. Many factors contribute to mental health problems, including:

- Biological factors, such as genes, physical illness, injury, or brain chemistry
- Life experiences, such as trauma or a history of abuse
- Family history of mental health problems

Helping Individuals with Mental Health Problems

Myth: There is no hope for people with mental health problems. Once a friend or family member develops mental health problems, he or she will never recover.
Fact: Studies show that people with mental health problems can get better with proper treatment, and many recover completely. Recovery refers to the process in which people are able to live, work, learn, and participate fully in their communities. There are more treatments, services, and community support systems than ever before, and they work.

Myth: Therapy and self-help are a waste of time. Why bother when you can just take a pill?
Fact: Treatment for mental health problems varies depending on the individual and could include medication, therapy, or both. Many individuals work with a support system during the healing and recovery process.

Myth: I can't do anything for a person with a mental health problem.
Fact: Friends and loved ones can make a big difference. Only 38 percent of

adults with diagnosable mental health problems and less than 20 percent of children and adolescents receive needed treatment. Friends and family can be important influences to help someone get the treatment and services they need by:

- Reaching out and letting them know you are available to help
- Helping them access mental health services
- Learning and sharing the facts about mental health, especially if you hear something that isn't true
- Treating them with respect, just as you would anyone else
- Refusing to define them by their diagnosis or using labels such as "crazy"

Myth: Prevention doesn't work. It is impossible to prevent mental illnesses.

Fact: Prevention of mental, emotional, and behavioral disorders focuses on addressing known risk factors such as exposure to trauma that can affect the chances that children, youth, and young adults will develop mental health problems. Promoting the social-emotional well-being of children and youth leads to:

- Higher overall productivity
- Better educational outcomes
- Lower crime rates
- Stronger economies
- Lower health care costs
- Improved quality of life
- Increased lifespan
- Improved family life[1]

Notes

Chapter 11

1. KHOU.Com Staff, "Tropical Storm Allison." Last modified June 8, 2011. Accessed July 26, 2014. *http://www.khou.com/community/slide-shows/Photos-Tropical-Storm-Allison--121959284.html* .

Chapter 25

1. Fred K., Berger, MD. PubMed Health, "Psychosis." Last modified 24 February 2014. Accessed July 26, 2014. *http://www.ncbi.nlm.nih.gov/pubmedhealth/PMH0002520/* .
2. E. Fuller Torrey, *American Psychosis: How the Federal Government Destroyed the Mental Illness Treatment System*, (Oxford: Oxford University Press, 2013), 152.
3. Ibid., 163.
4. Insel, Thomas. National Institute of Mental Health, "Director's Update: Mental Disorders as Brain Disorders." Last modified April 23, 2013. Accessed July 26, 2014. *http://www.nimh.nih.gov/about/updates/2013/mental-disorders-as-brain-disorders-thomas-insel-at-tedxcaltech.shtml.*
5. Simon, Stacy. American Cancer Society, "Childhood Leukemia Survival Rates Improve Significantly." Last modified March 27, 2012. Accessed July 26, 2014. *http://www.cancer.org/cancer/news/news/childhood-leukemia-survival-rates-improve-significantly.*

Chapter 26

1. MentalHealth.gov, "Mental Health Myths and Facts." Accessed July 26, 2014. *www.mentalhealth.gov/basics/myths-facts/index.html.*

About the Author

Benny Malone is a highly trained and experienced counselor with a master of social work from the University of Houston. She also has more than two hundred hours of post-graduate work in professional counseling, special education, and education leadership.

Benny's experience includes serving the State of Texas Health and Human Services Department, evaluating licensed residential care facilities and writing training materials for state-wide employees.

As the director of guidance, counseling, and special programs for the Cypress-Fairbanks Independent School Distric in Houston, she supervised more than two hundred professional staff members, writing district-wide handbooks, training materials, and public information documents.

Previously published in *The American School Counselor*, Benny also contributed to *Implementing Comprehensive School Guidance Programs* in 2002. And she served as project manager for a major revision of the State of Texas school counselor handbook for the education agency.

Benny lives in Houston and is an active volunteer in her community, church, and counseling organization.

PsychoticRage.com